McGRAW-HILL

SCIENCE

Macmillan/McGraw-Hill Edition

Richard Moyer • Lucy Daniel • Jay Hackett
H. Prentice Baptiste • Pamela Stryker • JoAnne Vasquez

NATIONAL
GEOGRAPHIC
SOCIETY

On the Cover:
Gouldian finches are some of the most vividly colorful
birds on Earth. There are three varieties—the red-headed,
black-headed, and yellow-headed. Their native habitat is
the northern region of Australia. They are not as abundant
today as they once were, due to loss of habitat.

Mc
Graw
Hill **Macmillan**
McGraw-Hill

New York   **Farmington**

Program Authors

Dr. Lucy H. Daniel
Teacher, Consultant
Rutherford County Schools, North Carolina

Dr. Jay Hackett
Professor Emeritus of Earth Sciences
University of Northern Colorado

Dr. Richard H. Moyer
Professor of Science Education
University of Michigan-Dearborn

Dr. H. Prentice Baptiste
Professor of Science and Multicultural Education
New Mexico State University
Las Cruces, New Mexico

Pamela Stryker, M.Ed.
Elementary Educator and Science Consultant
Eanes Independent School District
Austin, Texas

Dr. JoAnne Vasquez
Elementary Science Education Consultant
Mesa Public Schools, Arizona
NSTA Past President

RFB&D 〔◔〕
learning through listening

Students with print disabilities may be eligible to obtain an accessible, audio version of the pupil edition of this textbook. Please call Recording for the Blind & Dyslexic at 1-800-221-4792 for complete information.

NATIONAL GEOGRAPHIC SOCIETY
Washington, D.C.

The features in this textbook entitled "Invitation to Science," "Amazing Stories," and "People in Science," as well as the unit openers, were developed in collaboration with the National Geographic Society's School Publishing Division.

Macmillan/McGraw-Hill
A Division of The McGraw·Hill Companies

Published by Macmillan/McGraw-Hill, of McGraw-Hill Education, a division of The McGraw-Hill Companies, Inc., Two Penn Plaza, New York, New York 10121.

Printed in the United States of America

ISBN 0-02-280056-5 / 3

1 2 3 4 5 6 7 8 9 058 07 06 05 04 03 02

Teacher Reviewers

Peoria, IL
Rolling Acres Middle School
Gail Truho

Rockford, IL
Rockford Public Schools
Dr. Sharon Wynstra
Science Coordinator

Newark, NJ
Alexander Street School
Cheryl Simeonidis

Albuquerque, NM
Jackie Costales
Science Coordinator, Montgomery Complex

Poughkeepsie, NY
St. Peter's School
Monica Crolius

Columbus, OH
St. Mary's School
Linda Cotter
Joby Easley

Keizer, OR
Cummings Elementary
Deanna Havel

McMinnville, OR
McMinnville School District
Kristin Ward

Salem, OR
Fruitland Elementary
　Mike Knudson

Four Corners Elementary
　Bethany Ayers
　Sivhong Hanson
　Cheryl Kirkelie
　Julie Wells

Salem-Keizer Public Schools
　Rachael Harms
　Sue Smith,
　Science Specialist

Yoshikai Elementary
　Joyce Davenport

Norristown, PA
St. Teresa of Avila
Fran Fiordimondo

Pittsburgh, PA
Chartiers Valley Intermediate School
Rosemary Hutter

Memphis, TN
Memphis City Schools
Quincy Hathorn
District Science Facilitator

Life Science

Consultants

Dr. Carol Baskin
University of Kentucky
Lexington, KY

Dr. Joe W. Crim
University of Georgia
Athens, GA

Dr. Marie DiBerardino
Allegheny University of
Health Sciences
Philadelphia, PA

Dr. R. E. Duhrkopf
Baylor University
Waco, TX

Dr. Dennis L. Nelson
Montana State University
Bozeman, MT

Dr. Fred Sack
Ohio State University
Columbus, OH

Dr. Martin VanDyke
Denver, CO

Dr. E. Peter Volpe
Mercer University
Macon, GA

Earth Science

Consultants

Dr. Clarke Alexander
Skidaway Institute of
Oceanography
Savannah, GA

Dr. Suellen Cabe
Pembroke State University
Pembroke, NC

Dr. Thomas A. Davies
Texas A & M University
College Station, TX

Dr. Ed Geary
Geological Society of America
Boulder, CO

Dr. David C. Kopaska-Merkel
Geological Survey of Alabama
Tuscaloosa, AL

Physical Science

Consultants

Dr. Bonnie Buratti
Jet Propulsion Lab
Pasadena, CA

Dr. Shawn Carlson
Society of Amateur Scientists
San Diego, CA

Dr. Karen Kwitter
Williams College
Williamstown, MA

Dr. Steven Souza
Williamstown, MA

Dr. Joseph P. Straley
University of Kentucky
Lexington, KY

Dr. Thomas Troland
University of Kentucky
Lexington, KY

Dr. Josephine Davis Wallace
University of North Carolina
Charlotte, NC

Consultant for Primary Grades

Donna Harrell Lubcker
East Texas Baptist University
Marshall, TX

Teacher Panelists

Newark, NJ
First Avenue School
Jorge Alameda
Concetta Cioci
Neva Galasso
Bernadette Kazanjian-reviewer
Toby Marks
Janet Mayer-reviewer
Maria Tutela

Brooklyn, NY
P.S. 31
  Janet Mantel
  Paige McGlone
  Madeline Pappas
  Maria Puma-reviewer
P.S. 217
  Rosemary Ahern
  Charles Brown
  Claudia Deeb-reviewer
  Wendy Lerner
P.S. 225
  Christine Calafiore
  Annette Fisher-reviewer

P.S. 250
  Melissa Kane
P.S. 277
  Erica Cohen
  Helena Conti
  Anne Marie Corrado
  Deborah Scott-DiClemente
  Jeanne Fish
  Diane Fromhartz
  Tricia Hinz
  Lisa Iside
  Susan Malament
  Joyce Menkes-reviewer
  Elaine Noto
  Jean Pennacchio
Jeffrey Hampton
Mwaka Yavana

Elmont, NY
Covert Avenue School
Arlene Connelly

Mt. Vernon, NY
Holmes School
Jennifer Cavallaro
Lou Ciofi
George DiFiore
Brenda Durante
Jennifer Hawkins-reviewer
Michelle Mazzotta
Catherine Moringiello
Mary Jane Oria-reviewer
Lucille Pierotti
Pia Vicario-reviewer

Ozone Park, NY
St. Elizabeth School
Joanne Cocchiola-reviewer
Helen DiPietra-reviewer
Barbara Kingston
Madeline Visco

St. Albans, NY
Orvia Williams

UNIT F

Physical Science

Looking at Matter and Energy PAGE F1

As you study science, you will learn many new words. You will read about many new ideas. Read these pages. They will help you understand this book.

1. The **Vocabulary** list has all the new words you will learn in the lesson. The page numbers tell you where the words are taught.

2. The name tells you what the lesson is about.

3. **Get Ready** uses the picture on the page to help you start thinking about the lesson.

4. This **Process Skill** is used in the Explore Activity.

5. The **Explore Activity** is a hands-on way to learn about the lesson.

As you read a lesson, follow these three steps. They will help you to understand what you are reading.

1. This box contains the **Main Idea** of the lesson. Keep the main idea of the lesson in mind as you read.

2. **Before Reading** Read the large red question before you read the page. Try to answer this question from what you already know.

3. **During Reading** Look for new **Vocabulary** words in yellow. Look at the pictures. They will help you understand what you are reading.

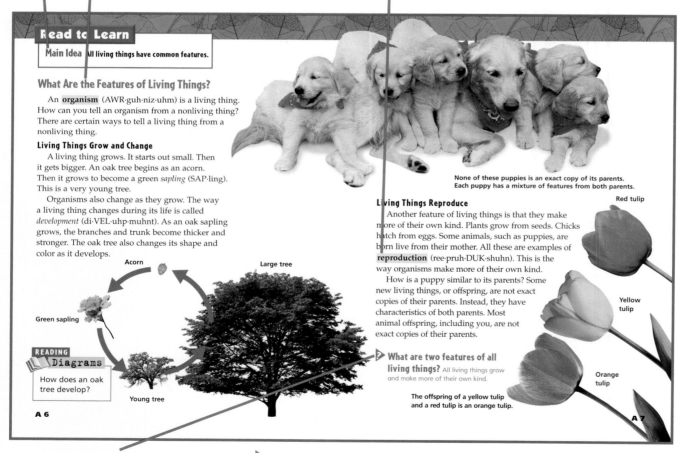

Read to Learn

Main Idea All living things have common features.

What Are the Features of Living Things?

An **organism** (AWR·guh·niz·uhm) is a living thing. How can you tell an organism from a nonliving thing? There are certain ways to tell a living thing from a nonliving thing.

Living Things Grow and Change

A living thing grows. It starts out small. Then it gets bigger. An oak tree begins as an acorn. Then it grows to become a green *sapling* (SAP·ling). This is a very young tree.

Organisms also change as they grow. The way a living thing changes during its life is called *development* (di·VEL·uhp·muhnt). As an oak sapling grows, the branches and trunk become thicker and stronger. The oak tree also changes its shape and color as it develops.

Acorn

Large tree

Green sapling

READING
Diagrams

How does an oak tree develop?

Young tree

A 6

None of these puppies is an exact copy of its parents. Each puppy has a mixture of features from both parents.

Living Things Reproduce

Another feature of living things is that they make more of their own kind. Plants grow from seeds. Chicks hatch from eggs. Some animals, such as puppies, are born live from their mother. All these are examples of **reproduction** (ree·pruh·DUK·shuhn). This is the way organisms make more of their own kind.

How is a puppy similar to its parents? Some new living things, or offspring, are not exact copies of their parents. Instead, they have characteristics of both parents. Most animal offspring, including you, are not exact copies of their parents.

▷ **What are two features of all living things?** All living things grow and make more of their own kind.

The offspring of a yellow tulip and a red tulip is an orange tulip.

Red tulip

Yellow tulip

Orange tulip

A 7

4. **After Reading** ▷ This arrow points to a question. It will help you check that you understand what you have read. Try to answer the question before you go to the next large red question.

UNIT F

Looking at Matter and Energy

NATIONAL GEOGRAPHIC

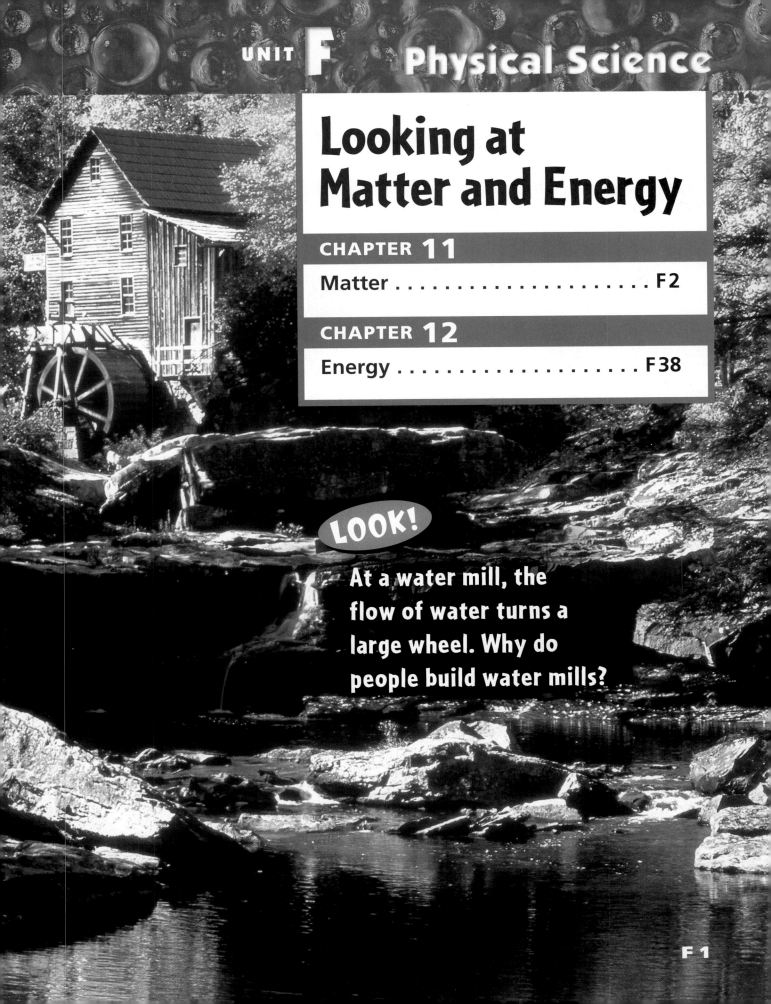

Looking at Matter and Energy

LOOK!

At a water mill, the flow of water turns a large wheel. Why do people build water mills?

CHAPTER 11

Matter

Did You Ever Wonder?

How can you tell different vegetables from one
another? Each vegetable has its own color, shape,
feel, and taste. Some even have a certain smell.
You can describe objects by their properties. What
property do you think a scale measures?

F 2

LESSON 1

Properties of Matter

Get Ready

Have you ever tried to stuff too many books into your book bag? The book bag has only so much room. Books take up space. Papers and pencils do, too. Do all objects take up space?

Process Skill

You experiment when you perform a test to support or disprove a hypothesis.

Explore Activity

Which Object Takes Up More Space?

Materials

plastic cup

water

markers

piece of clay

classroom objects

Procedure

1 Measure Half-fill the cup with water. Use a marker to mark the water level on the outside of the cup.

2 Observe Place the clay in the cup. What happens? Mark the new water level. Use a different color.

3 Predict Look at other objects. Which one will raise the water level most? Record your prediction.

4 Experiment Add one object at a time to the cup. Mark the new water level each time. Use a different color.

Drawing Conclusions

1 How did the size of the objects affect the water level?

2 Infer Which object takes up the most space? How do you know?

3 Going Further: Experiment What will happen to the water level in the cup if you change the shape of the clay?

Main Idea Matter is anything that takes up space and has mass.

How Do We Describe Matter?

Water, clay, rocks, and trees are all examples of **matter** (MAT·uhr). Matter is anything that takes up space and has mass. You are made of matter. This book and your pencil are, too. Every object you can name is made of matter.

The world is full of many kinds of matter. How do we tell them apart? Matter can be described by **properties** (PRAHP·uhr·teez). A property is any characteristic of matter that you can observe.

You can observe some properties with your sense of sight. You can observe color, size, and shape. You can also observe texture and luster. *Texture* (TEKS·chuhr) is how an object feels when you touch it. *Luster* (LUS·tuhr) is how an object shines in the light.

Observations of Matter

Object	dime
Color(s)	silver
Size	fits in hand
Shape	a thin circle
Texture	hard and bumpy
Flexibility	does not bend
Luster	shiny

READING Charts

1. What are some properties shown in the chart?

2. How could you make a chart like this for the other objects shown here? Try it.

Volume and Mass

Some objects take up more space than others. An object that takes up more space has a greater **volume** (VAHL·yewm). Volume is how much space an object takes up. The beach ball has a greater volume than the bowling ball. The bowling ball has a greater volume than the small rubber ball.

Another way to describe objects is by their **mass**. Mass is how much matter is in an object. An object with a large mass feels heavy. An object with a small mass feels light. The bowling ball has more mass than the beach ball.

▷ **Which object has the most volume? The most mass?**

How Do You Measure Mass and Volume?

Larger objects do not always have more mass than smaller ones. The bowling ball is smaller than the beach ball. However, the bowling ball has a greater mass. How is that possible?

Matter is made of very tiny particles. In some objects the particles are close together. In other objects they are farther apart. The particles inside the bowling ball are packed together tightly. They are packed more tightly than those inside the beach ball. The bowling ball is made of more particles than the beach ball. It has more mass.

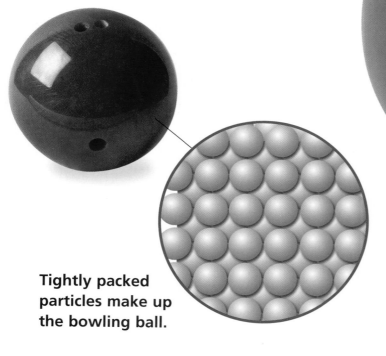

Tightly packed particles make up the bowling ball.

Particles of air are inside the beach ball. They are loosely packed.

This juice carton has a volume of two liters.

One unit used to measure mass is called the *gram*. One gram is the mass of about two small paper clips. A nickel has a mass of about five grams. You can use the letter *g* to stand for the word *gram*.

You can measure more massive objects in *kilograms*. One kilogram equals 1,000 grams. An eight-year-old has a mass close to 30 kilograms. You can use the letters *kg* to stand for this word.

One unit used to measure volume is the *liter*. You can use the letter *L* to stand for the word *liter*.

READING Draw Conclusions
Why does a bowling ball have more mass than a beach ball?

FOR SCHOOL OR HOME

Measuring Mass

1. **Predict** Gather some small objects. Predict the order of the objects from most mass to least mass.

2. **Measure** Measure the mass of each object. First, place the object on one side of a balance. Then, add paper clips to the other side until the two sides balance. Record the number of paper clips.

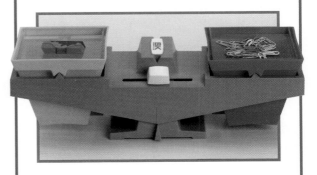

3. **Use Numbers** What is the mass of each object in grams? (Remember that two paper clips equals about one gram.)

F 9

How Are Mass and Weight Related?

The more mass an object has, the more it weighs. How are mass and weight different?

A good place to look for the answer is the Moon! If you visited the Moon, your mass would stay the same. The matter inside you would not change. However, you would weigh much less. This is because the weight of an object depends on the pull of gravity. Gravity is the force pulling two objects together. Your weight is the pull of gravity between you and Earth. The pull of gravity on the Moon is weaker than on Earth. Your weight here would be less.

Weight is an example of a force. Remember, a force is a push or a pull. Forces can be measured in units called *newtons*. If your mass is 25 kilograms, then your weight on Earth is 245 newtons.

▷ **How do mass and weight compare?**

Earth	Boy	Cat
Weight	235 N	58 N
Mass	24 kg	6 kg

Moon	Boy	Cat
Weight	40 N	9 N
Mass	24 kg	6 kg

Why It Matters

Matter is anything that takes up space and has mass. You can describe matter by naming its properties. You might describe your new sneakers to a friend or compare shirts at a store. Knowing an object's properties is important when you need to find a lost item.

Think and Write

1. List at least four physical properties of your favorite food.

2. What is the difference between mass and volume?

3. Does the largest object always have the greatest mass? Explain.

4. If your mass is 25 kilograms on Earth, what is your mass on the Moon? Explain your answer.

5. **Critical Thinking** Tanya has a rock, a measuring cup, and some water. How can she measure the volume of the rock?

L·I·N·K·S

SOCIAL STUDIES LINK

Conduct research. California and Texas are very large states. Each is home to more people than any of the other 48 states. Do all large states have more people than smaller states? Research the answer. Write down your findings. Share them with your classmates.

MATH LINK

Make a bar graph. The chart lists the masses of three living things. Which living thing has the most mass? Use this chart to make a bar graph. Remember to give your graph a title.

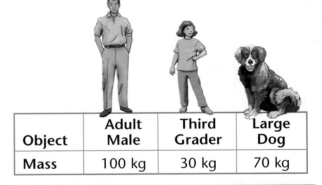

Object	Adult Male	Third Grader	Large Dog
Mass	100 kg	30 kg	70 kg

ART LINK

Draw a picture. Draw a picture of something you saw on your way to school. Label all of its properties.

TECHNOLOGY LINK

At the Computer Visit www.mhscience02.com for more links.

Comparing Solids, Liquids, and Gases

Get Ready

Do you see different kinds of matter all around you? Some matter is solid, like these leaves. What are some properties of solids? Some matter is liquid, like the drops of water on the leaves. What are some properties of liquids? The air is also matter. The air is a gas. What are some properties of gases?

Process Skill

You classify when you place things that share properties together in groups.

Explore Activity

How Can You Classify Matter?

Materials

plastic container of Oobleck

investigation tools

newspaper

safety goggles

Procedure: Design Your Own

BE CAREFUL! Wear goggles.

1. In your own words, define solids and liquids.

2. **Observe** Use your senses to describe Oobleck. How does it look? What does it feel like? Record your observations.

3. **Experiment** Use the tools given to you to experiment with Oobleck. What new things do you observe? Record your observations.

4. **Classify** Review your definitions of solids and liquids. Would you classify Oobleck as a solid or a liquid? Explain your answer.

Drawing Conclusions

1. **Communicate** What observations did you make about the properties of Oobleck?

2. How did you decide to classify Oobleck? What helped you make your decision?

3. **Going Further: Form a Hypothesis** Does Oobleck have different properties at different temperatures? Design an experiment to find out.

Main Idea Matter exists as solids, liquids, and gases.

How Can You Classify Matter?

Solids and liquids are two forms of matter. A third form of matter is gas. The forms of matter are also called states of matter. All states of matter take up space and have mass.

A sneaker is a **solid** (SAHL·id). A solid is matter that has a definite size and shape. *Definite* means it stays the same. Put a sneaker into a jar or box. It stays the same.

Juice is an example of a **liquid** (LIK·wid). A liquid is matter that has a definite volume. It does not have a definite shape. Pour juice into a glass. It will take on the shape of the glass.

A **gas** is matter that has no definite shape or volume. Gases take the shape of whatever container they are in. The air all around us is a gas.

This balloon is filled with a gas. The gas is helium.

The juice in this glass is a liquid.

This sneaker is a solid.

Remember that matter is made of particles. These particles are very, very small. In a solid the particles are packed closely together. They form a certain pattern. The pattern gives a solid its definite shape.

The particles in a liquid are close together. However, they do not form a pattern. The particles in a liquid have more energy. They are able to slide past one another. That is why liquids change shape.

The particles in a gas have even more energy. They spread out to fill a large container. They squeeze together to fit into a small container.

▷ **What do solids and liquids have in common?**

READING
Diagrams

1. How do the particles in a solid compare with the particles in a gas?

2. How would you describe the particles in a liquid?

Particles in Different States of Matter

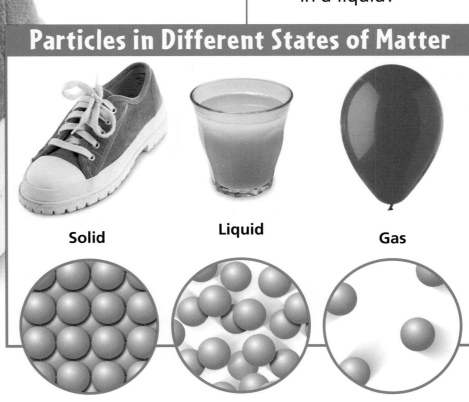

Solid   **Liquid**   **Gas**

How Can Matter Change?

Matter can change but still remain the same kind of matter. What happens when you cut a piece of paper? The paper looks different, but it is still made of the same particles. Cut paper into as many pieces as you like. It will still be paper!

The same is true when you make a wooden model. As you cut and sand the wood, its size and shape change. The wood is still wood. It is still made of the same particles.

A **physical change** (FIZ·i·kuhl CHAYNJ) is a change in how matter looks, but not in the kind of matter it is. The kind of matter stays the same. Cutting, folding, and sawing are examples of physical changes.

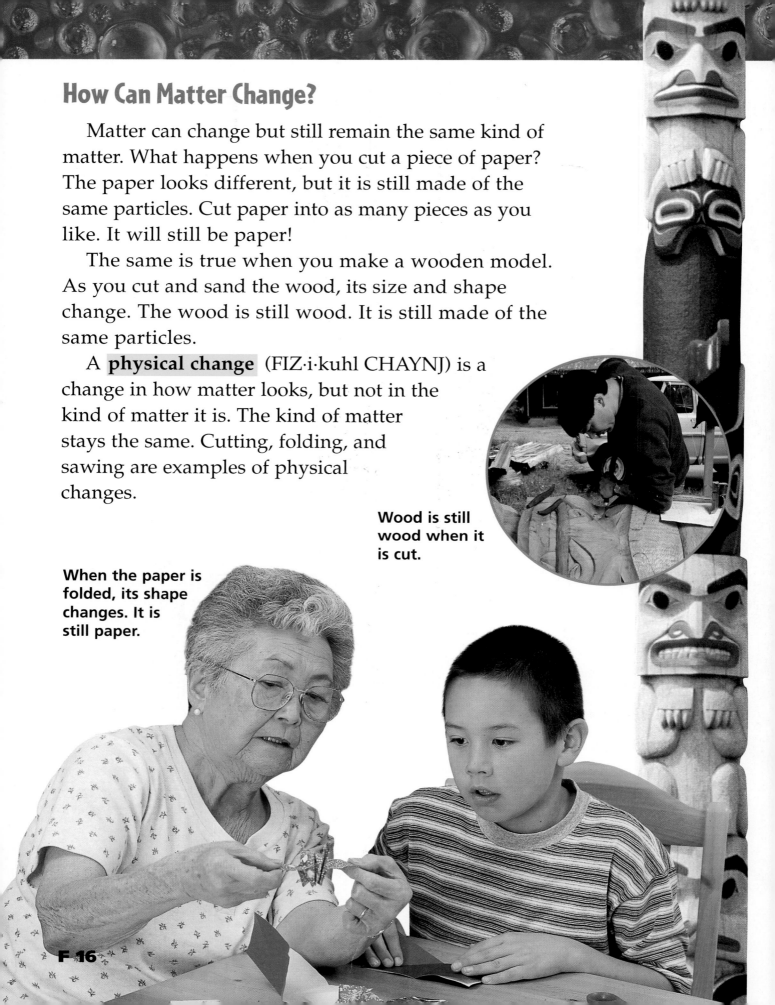

Wood is still wood when it is cut.

When the paper is folded, its shape changes. It is still paper.

Matter can change state. You can find water in the solid state, liquid state, or gas state. Water looks very different in each state, but it is still the same kind of matter.

Ice is the solid state of water. The particles in ice are close together. They do not move very much. When ice is heated, it *melts*. Melting is the change from solid to liquid. The particles gain energy and move faster.

Water can also change from a liquid to a gas. This happens when water *evaporates* (i·VAP·uh·rayts). The gas state of water is called water vapor. You cannot see water vapor. It is part of the air around you.

When water vapor cools, it loses energy and *condenses*. It becomes a liquid. When liquid water cools enough, it *freezes* into ice. Ice is a solid.

▶ **What is a physical change?**

READING

Charts

1. How can liquid water change to a solid?

2. How can liquid water change to a gas?

Changes of State

Melt
When ice melts, water changes from a solid to a liquid.

Freeze
When water freezes, liquid water changes to a solid.

Evaporate
When water evaporates, it changes into water vapor. You cannot see water vapor.

Condense
When water vapor in the air touches the cold glass, it condenses. You see the water drops on the outside of the glass.

Can You Mix Different Kinds of Matter Together?

When you mix different kinds of matter together, you may get a **mixture** (MIKS·chuhr). In a mixture the properties of each kind of matter do not change. Lemonade is a mixture of lemon juice and water.

Fruit salad is a mixture of many kinds of fruit. Pick out a piece of orange from a fruit salad. It will be just like any other orange piece.

Mixtures can be any combination of solids, liquids, and gases. Air is a mixture of different gases. Pour milk in your breakfast cereal. You have made a mixture of a liquid and a solid.

▷ **What is a mixture?**

What kinds of fruit make up this mixture?

How can you separate the rice, marbles, and paper clips in this mixture?

What Is a Solution?

Salt and water mix well together, forming a solution.

Sand and water do not mix well.

There are many kinds of mixtures. One kind of mixture is a **solution** (suh·LEW·shuhn). A solution forms when one or more kinds of matter are mixed evenly in another kind of matter.

Salt water is an example of a solution. Mix salt with water, and you cannot see the salt anymore. The salt is still there. If the water evaporates, the salt will be left behind.

Not all solids form solutions in water. Try to mix sand with water. The sand will just sink to the bottom. Some things fall to the bottom no matter how long you stir.

Some solutions contain no liquid at all! Air is a solution of different gases. Steel is a solution of several solids. Steel is used to make cars, bridges, and buildings.

READING Draw Conclusions
What do you need to make a solution?

Lemonade is a solution that contains water, lemon juice, and sugar.

Process Skill
BUILDER

SKILL Communicate

Making a Table

When you communicate, you share information with others. Scientists communicate what they learn from an experiment. They might tell people how they think the new information can be used. You can communicate by talking or by creating a drawing, chart, table, or graph.

Communicate what you know about the properties of solids, liquids, and gases. Look at the photograph on this page to help you answer the questions at right.

Procedure

1. **Observe** What states of matter do you see in the photograph?

2. What properties do these states have?

3. Draw a table like the one shown on this page.

4. **Communicate** Fill in the table with your observations.

Drawing Conclusions

Communicate Give an example of a solid, a liquid, and a gas. Write a sentence that tells about the shape and volume of each one.

Properties of Matter

States of Matter	Properties

Why It Matters

You eat many mixtures every day! Foods such as salad, pizza, and tacos are mixtures. You eat and drink solutions, too. Orange juice and hot cocoa are two examples of solutions. Can you think of other solutions you eat or drink?

Think and Write

1. Name three states of matter. Give an example of each.

2. What is a physical change?

3. How is a solution different from other kinds of mixtures?

4. **Communicate** How many ways can matter change state? Make a table.

5. **Critical Thinking** How would you separate salt from water?

L·I·N·K·S

ART LINK

Create a painting. Painters mix different colors together to make new ones. Use red, blue, and yellow paint to make some new colors. Then use these colors to paint a picture. Share the painting with your class.

SOCIAL STUDIES LINK

Write an article. In 1989 a ship spilled oil off the coast of Alaska. The oil collected on beaches and damaged wildlife. Workers were able to clean up the spill, however. Research the *Exxon Valdez* oil spill. Did the oil and water form a solution?

LITERATURE LINK

Read *A Ride Over the Serengeti* to learn how a boy and a girl used their knowledge of matter to make a safe landing. Try the activities at the end of the book.

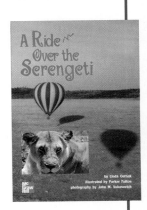

A Ride Over the Serengeti

by Linda Cernak
illustrated by Parker Fulton
photography by John M. Yukanovich

TECHNOLOGY LINK

At the Computer Visit **www.mhscience02.com** for more links.

POSITIVELY PLASTIC

Plastic is being rolled up at this factory.

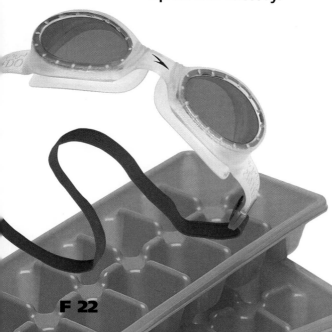

What comes in every color of the rainbow and can be found in almost every home in America? Plastic! We use plastic wrap to protect our foods. We put our leftovers in plastic containers. We put our garbage in plastic bags or plastic cans. We sit on plastic chairs, play with plastic toys, drink from plastic cups, and wash our hair with shampoo from plastic bottles! We know how useful it is, but exactly what is it?

Plastic doesn't grow in nature. It's made by mixing certain things together. We call it a produced or manufactured material. Plastic was first made in the 1850s from plants such as wood and cotton. However, the plastic was often soft and burned easily.

In the late 1920s, scientists began making usable plastics. Many modern plastics were invented in the 1930s.

NATIONAL GEOGRAPHIC

What are the compass and sail boat made of?

Today plastics are made from oil and natural gas. It's true! Most clear plastic starts out as thick, black oil. That hard plastic coating inside a cooking pan begins as natural gas!

Over the years hundreds of different plastics have been developed. Some are hard and strong. Some are soft and bendable. Some are clear. Some are many colored. There's a plastic for almost every need. Scientists continue to experiment with plastics. They hope to find even more ways to use them!

AT THE COMPUTER

Visit www.mhscience02.com to learn more about plastics.

What Did I Learn?

1. Plastic was first made from

A plants.
B animals.
C oil.
D natural gas.

2. According to the passage, plastics can be

F hard and strong.
G soft and bendable.
H clear or many colored.
J all of the above.

LESSON 3

Building Blocks of Matter

Vocabulary

metal, F26
element, F28
atom, F28
compound, F30
chemical change, F30

Get Ready

This large magnet is being lowered into a pile of junk. The magnet picks up some objects, but not others. If you used a magnet, what objects could you pick up?

Process Skill

You predict when you state possible results of an event or experiment.

F 24

Explore Activity

What Do Magnets Attract?

Materials

magnet

several objects

Procedure

1 Observe Look at your objects. What properties of the objects do you observe? Record your observations.

2 Predict Which objects will the magnet attract? Record your predictions.

3 Experiment Get a magnet from your teacher. Test your predictions. Hold a magnet over each object. Record the results.

Drawing Conclusions

1 Classify Use a table like the one below to identify objects the magnet attracts and those objects it does not attract.

2 What do the objects that a magnet attracts have in common? What do the objects that a magnet does not attract have in common?

3 Going Further: Predict What are some other objects a magnet might attract? Test your predictions.

Magnet attracts	Magnet does not attract

Main Idea Elements are the building blocks of matter.

What Are Metals?

Magnets attract some objects, but not others. Objects that a magnet attracts are made of certain **metals** (MET·uhlz). A metal is a hard, shiny material found in Earth's ground. There are many kinds of metals. Magnets attract the metal called iron, and other metals, too.

Anything that attracts metals has the property of *magnetism* (MAG·ni·tiz·uhm). Magnetism is the property that holds a magnet to your refrigerator.

Magnetism is very useful. Visit a junkyard. You can see magnetism at work. It is used to sort certain metals from other objects.

What Is a Magnet?

A magnet is an object that attracts iron and some other metals.

A rock called magnetite acts as a weak magnet.

The magnets you use are called permanent magnets. They are often made of iron or steel.

Do you need iron in your body? The answer is yes! You need to eat iron every day to stay healthy. You get iron from meats and dark green vegetables, such as spinach.

Iron is often mixed with other materials to make steel. Steel is strong and lasts a long time. It is used to build things such as bridges, railroads, and cars.

Other metals include gold, silver, copper, and aluminum (a·LEW·muh·nuhm). Each metal has its own properties. Copper and aluminum are light and soft. We use copper to make pipes. We use aluminum to make airplanes. Gold is soft, yellow, and very shiny. Silver is shiny, too. We often use gold and silver to make jewelry.

▶ **What properties do metals have?**

Steel is used to make trains.

Spinach contains the metal iron, which is important to good health.

Gold is used to make jewelry because it is soft and shiny.

Aluminum is strong and light, so it is used to make canoes.

F 27

What Are the Building Blocks of Matter?

The metals iron, gold, silver, and copper are **elements** (EL·uh·muhnts). Elements are the building blocks of matter. There are more than 100 different elements. They make up all the matter in the world. Some elements, such as iron and copper, are solids. Other elements are found as liquids. Still others, such as helium (HEE·lee·uhm), are gases.

Each element has its own properties. Elements join together in different ways. They form everything on Earth.

All elements are made of **atoms** (AT·uhmz). An atom is the smallest particle of matter. It is too small to see with your eyes. The atoms that make up one element are all alike. They are different from the atoms of other elements.

Long ago, people thought the only elements were air, water, fire, and earth. Today we know these are not elements.

The element neon is used to light signs. Neon is a gas.

The element helium is used to fill these balloons.

For example, water can break apart into two gases. These gases are hydrogen and oxygen. Both of these gases are elements.

Do you think wood is an element? If wood is heated, it gives off gases. It also produces a solid, black substance. This substance is called carbon. Carbon is an element. If carbon is heated, it only gets hotter.

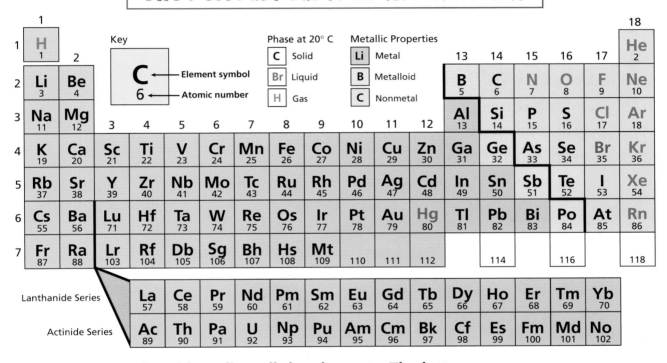

> **What is an element?**

The Periodic Table of the Elements

Key

C ← Element symbol
6 ← Atomic number

Phase at 20° C
- C Solid
- Br Liquid
- H Gas

Metallic Properties
- Li Metal
- B Metalloid
- C Nonmetal

1	2	3	4	5	6	7	8	9	10	11	12	13	14	15	16	17	18
H 1																	He 2
Li 3	Be 4											B 5	C 6	N 7	O 8	F 9	Ne 10
Na 11	Mg 12											Al 13	Si 14	P 15	S 16	Cl 17	Ar 18
K 19	Ca 20	Sc 21	Ti 22	V 23	Cr 24	Mn 25	Fe 26	Co 27	Ni 28	Cu 29	Zn 30	Ga 31	Ge 32	As 33	Se 34	Br 35	Kr 36
Rb 37	Sr 38	Y 39	Zr 40	Nb 41	Mo 42	Tc 43	Ru 44	Rh 45	Pd 46	Ag 47	Cd 48	In 49	Sn 50	Sb 51	Te 52	I 53	Xe 54
Cs 55	Ba 56	Lu 71	Hf 72	Ta 73	W 74	Re 75	Os 76	Ir 77	Pt 78	Au 79	Hg 80	Tl 81	Pb 82	Bi 83	Po 84	At 85	Rn 86
Fr 87	Ra 88	Lr 103	Rf 104	Db 105	Sg 106	Bh 107	Hs 108	Mt 109	110	111	112		114		116		118

Lanthanide Series

La 57	Ce 58	Pr 59	Nd 60	Pm 61	Sm 62	Eu 63	Gd 64	Tb 65	Dy 66	Ho 67	Er 68	Tm 69	Yb 70

Actinide Series

Ac 89	Th 90	Pa 91	U 92	Np 93	Pu 94	Am 95	Cm 96	Bk 97	Cf 98	Es 99	Fm 100	Md 101	No 102

This is the periodic table. It lists all the elements. The letter or letters in each box stand for the name of the element.

The tusks of a walrus contain calcium. Calcium is an element.

What Happens When Elements Join Together?

How do about 100 elements form all the materials on Earth? Elements can join together to form **compounds** (KAHM·powndz). A compound may form when you put two or more elements together. Compounds have very different properties from the elements they are made of.

Some compounds are made of just two elements. Have you seen rust on an old fence? Rust is a compound made of the two elements iron and oxygen.

When a compound forms, a **chemical change** (KEM·i·kuhl CHAYNJ) has taken place. Chemical changes are changes in the matter itself. In a chemical change, you start with one kind of matter. You end with another kind of matter.

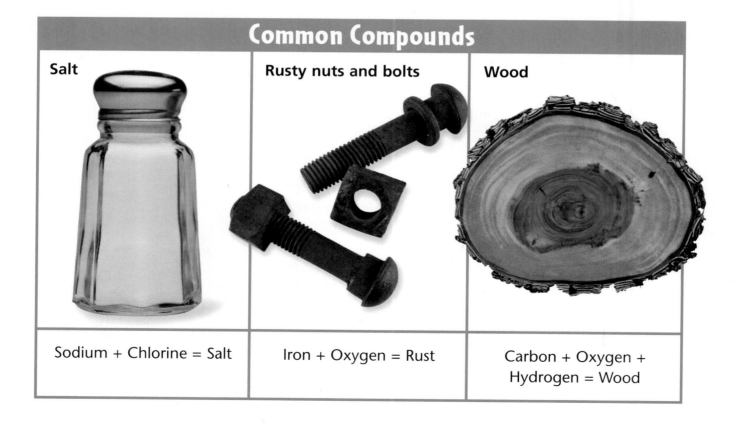

Common Compounds

Salt	Rusty nuts and bolts	Wood
Sodium + Chlorine = Salt	Iron + Oxygen = Rust	Carbon + Oxygen + Hydrogen = Wood

You observe chemical changes every day. When wood burns, it produces gases and ash. This is a chemical change. Iron changing into rust is also a chemical change. Rust is very different from iron. It is softer, and it peels.

Cooking uses lots of chemical changes. Cake batter changes when you bake it. You know it has changed because it feels and tastes different. When you eat the cake, your body breaks it down. Then your body uses its energy. These, too, are chemical changes.

A chemical change is happening in the lighted match. The wood is combining with oxygen in the air to form new kinds of matter.

Chemical changes happen when plants make food. They change water and carbon dioxide into food.

▶ **What are two common chemical changes?**

Heat causes a chemical change in the dough. It changes into bread.

How Do Chemical Changes and Physical Changes Compare?

Remember that folding and tearing are physical changes. Freezing and melting are, too. Matter looks different after a physical change, but the kind of matter stays the same.

In a chemical change, the kind of matter changes. Look for one material going away and a new material forming. That is a sign of a chemical change. Other signs are burning, forming bubbles, and forming new colors.

READING Draw Conclusions

How can you tell a chemical change from a physical change?

Toasting a marshmallow is a chemical change.

Chemical changes happen when a tomato becomes ripe.

Melting is a physical change.

Cutting paper is making a physical change.

F 32

Why It Matters

Everything in the world is made of elements. Elements are the building blocks of matter. You need some elements and compounds to live and grow. Others make life easier or more fun. Some can be dangerous!

Your body changes as you grow. Both physical changes and chemical changes take place inside you every day.

Visit **www.mhscience02.com** to do a research project on physical and chemical changes.

Think and Write

1. What kinds of objects does a magnet attract?

2. What is an element?

3. What is the difference between a physical change and a chemical change?

4. How are elements different from compounds?

5. Critical Thinking Two clear liquids are mixed together. Bubbles and a green powder form. What kind of change is this? Explain.

L·I·N·K·S

WRITING LINK

Research the gold rush. In the 1840s gold was discovered in California. Many people headed west to dig for gold and to become rich. This event was called the gold rush. Research how it changed California. Write down your findings.

MATH LINK

Make a bar graph. Scientists discovered elements over the years. The chart shows the number of known elements in different years. Make a bar graph that shows this information.

Year	1800	1850	1900	1950	2000
Known elements	33	57	81	96	109

LITERATURE LINK

Read _I Can't Believe My Eyes_ to see some extraordinary photographs of ordinary things. Create a picture like those in the book. Try the activities at the end of the book.

TECHNOLOGY LINK

At the Computer Visit **www.mhscience02.com** for more links.

GLASS is GREAT!

Why is this speedboat made of fiberglass?

What can be spun into threads finer than a spider's web? What can be molded into huge mirrors that weigh as much as five elephants? What can be stronger than steel or crumble like a cracker? The answer is glass!

The simplest glass is made of a mixture of sand and small amounts of other materials, such as soda ash and limestone. The mixture is melted, then shaped. The glass hardens as it cools.

We use many kinds of glass. One kind is very strong glass, called safety glass. It is used in car windows. Safety glass is hard to break.

When it does break, it shatters into small pieces with dull edges. Another kind of glass, called fiberglass, is made of thin glass fibers. Each fiber is many times thinner than a human hair. Some boats are made of fiberglass because it is strong and light. Fiberglass is also used in firefighters' suits because it does not burn and it washes easily.

Glass is amazing for another reason. It can be recycled. Americans recycle 13 million glass bottles and jars every day. They are melted and formed into new glass products.

Objects made from glass

A glassblower shapes soft, hot glass.

This is where glass is stored when it is waiting to be recycled.

What Did I Learn?

1. Glass can be
   A spun into threads.
   B stronger than steel.
   C molded into huge mirrors.
   D all of the above.
2. Thin glass fibers are used in
   F fiberglass.
   G safety glass.
   H recycled glass.
   J molded glass.

Visit www.mhscience02.com to learn more about glass.

Chapter 11 Review

Vocabulary

Fill in each blank with the best word or words from the list.

chemical change, F30
compound, F30
element, F28
gas, F14
liquid, F14
mass, F7
metal, F26
physical change, F16
physical property, F6
solid, F14
volume, F7

1. The amount of space an object takes up is its _____.

2. Size and color are examples of a(n) _____.

3. Grams are one unit of measurement for _____.

4. A shiny material found in Earth is a(n) _____.

5. A building block of matter is a(n) _____.

6. No new kinds of matter are formed in a(n) _____.

7. New kinds of matter are formed in a(n) _____.

The states of matter are:

8. _____

9. _____

10. _____.

Test Prep

11. What does NOT describe the physical properties of your science book?

  A smooth

  B hard

  C soft

  D rectangular shape

12. Matter that does not have a definite shape or volume is a(n) _____.

  F gas

  G solid

  H liquid

  J element

13. Which is an example of a solution?

  A marbles and paper clips

  B salt mixed in water

  C fruit salad

  D sand and water

14. Which of the following is a physical change?

  F a cake baking

  G ice melting

  H metal rusting

  J wood burning

15. One example of an element is _____.

 A wood

 B fruit salad

 C rust

 D hydrogen

Concepts and Skills

16. Reading in Science How can you tell the difference between a mixture and a compound?

17. Process Skills: Communicate Draw diagrams that show the differences among solids, liquids, and gases. Write a brief explanation of each diagram.

18. Critical Thinking One element that makes up salt is a poisonous gas. Why do you think that salt does not poison us?

Salt

Chlorine gas— a poisonous green gas

19. Product Ads You may have seen ads on television that show people sitting on clouds. What properties of matter have the advertisers ignored? Write a sentence to explain your answer.

20. Scientific Methods Metals are good carriers of heat. They heat up quickly. Do metals also cool off quickly? Write a hypothesis. Describe how you would test your idea.

F 37

CHAPTER 12

Energy

Did You Ever Wonder?

Have you ever experienced a power outage? During
a blackout the lights go out. It is totally dark! Electric
machines stop working. Electricity is a form of energy
we use every day. What is energy? What are some
other forms of energy?

F 38

How Heat Travels

Vocabulary

heat, F42
temperature, F43
degree, F43
conductor, F46
insulator, F46

Get Ready

Could you fry an egg on the sidewalk? In Oatman, Arizona, they try! Oatman has a sidewalk egg-frying contest every year on the Fourth of July. Sidewalks can get very hot in the sunlight. Sand at the beach and metals can, too. Other things, such as water, stay cooler. Why do some things warm up more than others?

Process Skill

You experiment when you perform a test to support or disprove a hypothesis.

Explore Activity

How Does Heat Affect Different Materials?

Materials

soil

water

2 foam cups

2 thermometers

heat source (sunlight or lamp)

Procedure

1. Fill one cup with water. Fill the other cup with an equal amount of soil.

2. **Measure** Use two thermometers to measure the temperature of the soil and the water. Record the measurements.

3. **Predict** Predict how hot the soil and water will get if they are left in a warm place for 15 minutes. Record your prediction.

4. **Experiment** Place the soil and water near a heat source. Make sure each cup is the same distance from the heat source. Record the temperature every 5 minutes for 15 minutes.

5. **Use Numbers** Find the difference between the first and last readings of each thermometer. To do this, subtract the first measurement you made from the last measurement you made.

Drawing Conclusions

1. Which cup warmed up more? Were your predictions correct?

2. **Infer** Why is it important to place the soil and water an equal distance from the heat source?

3. **Going Further: Experiment** Try this activity using gravel, sand, or salt.

Main Idea Heat is a form of energy that makes things warmer.

How Do Things Get Warmer?

Rub your hands together quickly. What happens? Your hands warm up. Why did this happen? The energy from your moving hands changed to **heat** . Heat is a form of energy that makes matter warmer.

The Sun is Earth's main source of heat. Fire and light bulbs also produce heat. The coils inside an oven or toaster produce heat, too.

Heat can move in different ways. It can move through solids, liquids, and gases. Heat can even move through space. This helps us because space lies between Earth and the Sun.

READING Diagrams

How does the soup in the pot get warmer?

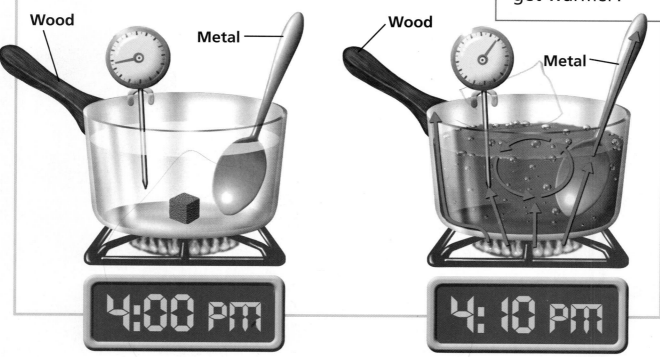

Wood   Metal

Wood   Metal

4:00 PM   4:10 PM

A thermometer measures **temperature** (TEM·puhr·uh·chuhr). Temperature is a measure of how warm or cold something is. The units of temperature are called **degrees** (di·GREEZ). The symbol for degree is °. It is a tiny, raised circle.

Some materials need more energy to cause the same change in their temperature. At the beach you will find sand and water. Both are under the same heat source, the Sun. The sand gets very hot, but the water stays much cooler. The water needs more energy to cause the same change in temperature.

The coils in a toaster get very hot. Heat moves into the food to toast it.

▶ **What is temperature?**

Why would you go for a swim on a hot day?

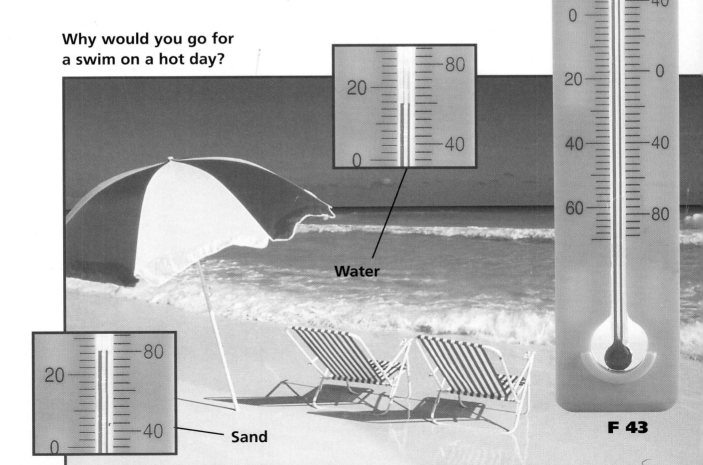

Water

Sand

How Does Heat Change Matter?

You can't see heat. You cannot hold it in your hand, either. However, you can see how heat changes matter.

Look at the road. The Sun heated it day after day. This made the road expand. To expand means to get bigger. The road expanded so much that cracks formed.

Why did this happen? Remember that matter is made of particles. Adding heat makes the particles move faster. It also causes them to move farther apart. This raises the temperature and makes the matter expand.

When matter loses heat, its particles slow down. They also move closer together. Losing heat is the same as cooling. Matter contracts as it cools. To contract means to get smaller.

You learned that a thermometer measures how warm or cold something is. How does it do this? A thermometer is a glass tube filled with a liquid. The liquid expands and contracts to show different temperatures.

When heat makes the liquid expand, the liquid rises up the tube.

Roads may expand and crack in hot weather.

When a thermometer is in a warm place, the liquid in the thermometer rises. When the air around the thermometer loses heat, the liquid in the thermometer falls. The level tells you the temperature.

Heat always flows from warmer objects to cooler ones. Heat flows from a warm room to a cold ice pop. The particles in the ice pop move faster and farther apart. The ice pop melts.

READING Sequence of Events
What happens to an ice pop when you take it from a freezer and later put it back?

QUICK LAB

FOR SCHOOL OR HOME

Expand and Contract

1. Stretch the opening of a balloon over a soda bottle.

2. **Observe** Place the bottle in a bucket of warm water. What happens to the balloon?

3. **Observe** Move the bottle to a bucket of cold water. What happens to the balloon?

4. **Communicate** Make a diagram to explain the changes in the balloon.

How Can You Control the Flow of Heat?

Why are cooking pots made of metals such as iron and aluminum? The answer is that heat moves quickly through metals. The heat moves from the stove to the metal pot. The pot gets warm.

Materials such as metals are good **conductors** (kuhn·DUK·tuhrz). A conductor is a material that heat moves through easily.

Heat does not move quickly through some other materials, such as wool, cotton, and fur. These materials are called **insulators** (IN·suh·lay·tuhrz). An insulator is a material that heat does not move through easily.

Cooking pots are made of conductors.

Insulation keeps heat inside the house.

In cold weather people need to stay warm. This boy is wearing clothing that traps heat.

Winters in the north get very cold. How do animals that live there stay warm? Good insulators cover their bodies. Animals such as the walrus have layers of fat under their skin. Fat is an excellent insulator. Bears have very thick hair that helps trap heat inside the animal's body.

This Red-Eyed Tree Frog can live only in warm places, such as the rain forest. In the cold its thin skin would lose heat. It would die.

▷ **How are conductors and insulators used?**

Walruses

Brown bears

Insulators help these animals stay warm in cold places.

How Can Energy Change?

Heat is a form of energy. Energy changes from one form to another. Many forms of energy can change into heat. For example, rub your hands together. Some of the energy of moving your hands changes into heat. For the same reason, sawing wood or bending wire produces heat. Fuel, such as wood or gasoline, has energy locked in it. When fuel is burned, heat is given off.

Food is fuel for your body. As your body uses food, heat is produced. That's why your body has a certain temperature.

▷ **What is an example of energy changing form?**

Burning wood gives off heat.

Cutting wood makes the saw hot. Some of the energy moving the saw changes to heat.

It is very warm inside your body. Your body heat comes from the energy in your food.

Lesson Review

Why It Matters

Your body needs food. As your body uses food, it produces heat. It uses this energy from food to keep the same body temperature. Not all animals can do this. Some animals get heat from outside their bodies. Their body temperature changes with the temperature of the surroundings. Snakes will warm themselves in the sunlight. When they get warm, they move into the shade.

Think and Write

1. What is heat? Give an example of an object that gives off heat.

2. How does a thermometer work?

3. Name a good conductor. Name a good insulator.

4. What happens to the particles of matter when matter is heated? Draw a diagram.

5. **Critical Thinking** Why do people use foam cups when they drink hot chocolate?

L·I·N·K·S

WRITING LINK

Write an expository paragraph. Sometimes the weather stays very hot for many days. This is called a heat wave. Ask adults about the worst heat wave they remember. Write down their answers. Share them with your class.

SOCIAL STUDIES LINK

Write a report. Some farm crops grow best at hot temperatures. Others grow best at cooler temperatures. Research the crops grown in your state. Find out why farmers grow these crops.

ART LINK

Make a model. Make a model that shows what happens when matter is heated. Use clay, felt, or cotton balls as the particles of matter. Present your model as a poster or diorama.

TECHNOLOGY LINK

At the Computer Visit **www.mhscience02.com** for more links.

SAVING ENERGY

Why is it important to save energy? Most of the energy we use comes from fossil fuels. Fossil fuels are burned to make electricity, heat buildings, and power cars. Burning destroys these fuels. Once they are gone, they are gone forever.

You can help! You can save energy and reduce your use of fossil fuels. This will make Earth's supply of fossil fuels last longer. It will decrease air pollution. You will save money, too.

There are many ways to save energy. Some are surprising. All are simple to do.

Solar calculator

- Turn out lights when you are not using them.
- Clean dust off light bulbs. Clean light bulbs work better than dirty ones.
- Don't use batteries when other choices are available. Try a solar calculator that runs on light. Play with toys that do not run on batteries.

- Saving hot water saves both water and energy. Don't waste water when you take a bath, wash your hands, or do the dishes.
- Don't keep refrigerators open for a long time. Think about what you want before you open the door.
- Don't turn the heat in your house too high in the winter. Stay warm by wearing a sweater.
- Use cars wisely. Take buses or trains when you can. Or walk or ride a bike.

It is up to everyone to use energy wisely. How many ways can you save energy?

How are these children saving energy?

AT THE COMPUTER

Visit www.mhscience02.com to learn more about saving energy.

What Did I Learn?

1. What can you conserve by saving electricity?

A aluminum
B trees
C fossil fuels
D batteries

2. Which of the following is a reason to save energy?

F decrease air pollution
G save money
H reduce use of fossil fuels
J all of the above

Vocabulary

opaque, F54
reflect, F55
refract, F56

How Light Travels

Get Ready

You depend on light every day. Sunlight in the morning tells you a new day has begun. Light allows you to see people and objects. Look at the picture shown here. Some things, such as the window and the vase, let light shine through. Other things, such as the wall, block the light.

What materials let light pass through them?

Process Skill

You predict when you state the possible results of an event or experiment.

F 52

Explore Activity

What Does Light Pass Through?

Materials

flashlight

classroom materials, such as paper, wax paper, plastic wrap, aluminum foil, large balloon

Procedure

1 Predict Look over your materials. Which materials will light pass through? Which materials will form shadows?

2 Experiment Hold each material in front of the lighted flashlight. Does light shine through the material? Do any shadows form? Record your observations.

3 Experiment Try changing the materials in some way. You may try folding the papers to make them thicker, or crumpling the plastic wrap. Repeat step 2 with the changed materials.

Drawing Conclusions

1 Classify Which materials did the light pass through? Which materials formed shadows? Make a list.

2 Did changing the materials change the results? Explain any changes you observed.

3 Going Further: Predict Use the materials to make a window hanging. Predict how the hanging will look when the only light comes from outside.

Main Idea Light travels in straight lines.

How Does Light Travel?

You see and use light every day. What is light? Light is a form of energy. Light is not matter, but it can make matter move or change.

Light comes from many different sources. The Sun and other stars, lightning, and fires are natural light sources. Light bulbs and candles are made by people.

Light travels in straight lines from its source. A beam of light is called a light ray.

Some materials let light rays pass through them easily. Air, glass, and some plastics are examples. Other materials block light rays. These materials are called **opaque** (oh·PAYK). Bricks, wood, metals, and many other materials are opaque. An opaque material will make a shadow when light is shined on it.

Are these objects opaque? How do you know?

Rays of light travel in straight lines from the Sun to Earth.

Put two or three mirrors together. You can see more reflections.

When light hits an object, some light **reflects** (ri·FLEKTS) off the object. *Reflect* means "bounce." You see an object because light reflected from the object enters your eye.

Mirrors reflect light very well. That's because mirrors are smooth and shiny. A light ray reflects off a mirror just like a table tennis ball bounces off a smooth table. Look at a mirror, and you will see your face. This is your reflection.

Most objects are not as smooth and shiny as a mirror. A light ray that hits something dull or rough bounces in lots of different directions. This is why you don't see your reflection when you look at most things.

A curved mirror reflects light in a different way from a flat mirror. It might stretch your reflection or turn it upside down.

READING **Sequence of Events**
Why do you see your reflection when you look in a mirror?

F 55

Why Does Light Bend?

Look at the spoon in the water. It looks as if the bottom was cut away from the top! In fact, this spoon is not cut at all.

Why does the spoon look broken? The light **refracts** (ri·FRAKTS) as it passes from air into water. To refract means to bend. The bending light rays make the spoon look as if it is broken.

Light also refracts as it passes between air and glass. This can be very useful. People can see better by looking through a piece of glass shaped the right way.

A light beam going from air into water.

▷ **Why does the spoon look broken in the water?**

A camera uses a lens to bend light and focus the light on the film.

Eyeglasses help people see better. Lenses work by refracting light.

Why Do You See Colors?

You might think that light from the Sun is yellow or white. In fact, it is a mixture of many colors! To show this, you can use a *prism* (PRIZ·uhm). A prism is a thick piece of glass that refracts light. The prism bends each color a different amount.

We see objects when light reflects off them. Most objects reflect some colors better than other colors. The colors that are not reflected are absorbed. An apple reflects red light and absorbs most of the other colors. A green leaf reflects green light. Blue paint reflects blue light. This is why we see colors.

▷ **What does a prism do to light?**

Sunlight

READING
Diagrams

Why does an apple look red?

Tiny drops of water in the air act like a prism. This forms a rainbow!

Sunlight

When a light ray enters a prism, the colors are bent in different amounts and break apart.

Process Skill
BUILDER

Controlling an Experiment

Variables are things in an experiment that can be changed to find answers to questions. For example, what if you wanted to answer the question "What affects how light bends in a liquid?" Here are some variables that could be changed.

- the kind of liquid
- the shape of the container
- the position of an object in the liquid

For a fair test, all of the variables in the experiment must remain the same except for one. There can be only one variable.

Variable	Control

Procedure

1 **Communicate** Take a close look at the containers in the picture. What differences do you see? These differences are variables. List all the variables you can. Use a table.

2 **Use Variables** Describe a fair test for each variable. For example, how would you test the shape of the container?

Drawing Conclusions

1 How many variables can you change in a fair test?

2 **Use Variables** Which one variable would you change to see its effect on the bending of light? Why?

Why It Matters

Light is everywhere in your world. You are using light as you are reading these words.

People use light to communicate. Traffic lights tell you when it is safe to cross the street. Light is used to make television shows and movies. How else do you use light?

Think and Write

1. Name three things that make light.

2. What kinds of objects make shadows?

3. When you look at an object that reflects light very well, what do you see?

4. **Use Variables** You want to know if sunlight fades paper. List the variables in the experiment.

5. **Critical Thinking** A magician says that she can bend a wand. She dips the wand in water. The wand looks bent. Explain how this trick works.

L·I·N·K·S

ART LINK

Create a sculpture. Use crayons, tissue paper, wax paper, and other materials. Be sure to use some opaque materials and some that let light through. Share your sculpture with your class.

MATH LINK

Measure length. Turn off the lights. Shine a flashlight on a ruler. Use another ruler to measure the length of the shadow. Measure shadows with the flashlight in different positions. Use the table to record your measurements. How does the flashlight position affect the shadow?

Position of flashlight	Length of shadow

TECHNOLOGY LINK

Science Newsroom CD ROM Choose *Time to Reflect* to learn how mirror reflections and light are related.

At the Computer Visit **www.mhscience02.com** for more links.

WAVES OF ENERGY

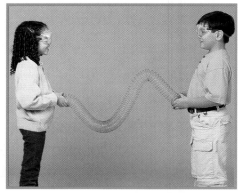

A spring toy can show how sound waves travel.

How does light get from the Sun to Earth? How does music get from the stage to the audience? They move the same way—in waves!

Light and sound are forms of energy. All waves carry energy, but they may carry it differently. Light and sound travel through different kinds of matter. For example, light waves can't move through walls, but sound waves can. That's why you can hear people talking in another room even though you can't see them. The energy of some waves is destructive. An earthquake produces seismic waves.

Sound travels in waves from the violin to your ear.

NATIONAL GEOGRAPHIC

Catch a wave. Ask a friend to stand a few feet away from you. Stretch a spring between you. Shake the spring to transfer energy to it. What happens? The spring bounces up and down in waves. When the waves reach your friend, they bounce back to you!

Light waves travel 300,000 kilometers (186,000 miles) per second! They can travel through a vacuum—a space without matter. That's why light from the Sun and distant stars can travel through space to Earth!

Light travels in straight lines.

What Did I Learn?

1. A spring toy can show how

   A energy waves travel.
   B an earthquake happens.
   C shadows are made.
   D sound makes an echo.

2. Light waves can travel through

   F walls.
   G a vacuum.
   H mountains.
   J wood.

AT THE COMPUTER

Visit www.mhscience02.com to learn more about light and sound waves.

Properties of Sound

Get Ready

Everyone waits quietly. There isn't a sound. Soon you hear the drums drumming. Then you hear the flutes singing. The band is here! At a parade you hear lots of music. What makes all of these sounds?

Process Skill

You experiment when you perform a test to support or disprove a hypothesis.

Explore Activity

How Can You Make Sounds?

Materials

paper strips, 10 cm (4 in.) wide

tape

scissors

straws

plastic rulers

Procedure: Design Your Own

1 Observe Hold a strip of paper at an end. Wave it. Describe what you hear.

2 Observe Flatten a straw. Cut a point on one end of the straw. Blow hard through that end. Describe what you hear.

3 Observe Hold a ruler on a desktop. Let half of the ruler reach over the edge. Tap that end. Describe what you hear.

4 Experiment Test ways to change the sound you made with each object. Try to make the sounds louder or softer, higher or lower. For example, try using strips of paper of different lengths.

Drawing Conclusions

1 What makes sounds?

2 How can you make a sound change?

3 Going Further: Experiment Make more sound makers out of other materials, such as string and paper cups. How can you change the sounds?

Main Idea Sounds can travel through all kinds of matter.

How Are Sounds Made?

To make a sound, you need to make something move. Put your hand to your throat, and speak. You can feel something moving inside. Tap the end of a ruler that you are holding over a desk. You hear it and see it move.

Sounds are made when an object **vibrates** (VIGH·brayts). To vibrate is to move back and forth quickly. Sometimes you can see an object vibrate. Pluck a guitar string. You might see it vibrate. Other times it may vibrate so fast you can't see it moving.

When a guitar string vibrates, it makes the air around it vibrate, too. Particles in the air move back and forth quickly.

You hear the ruler, and see it move.

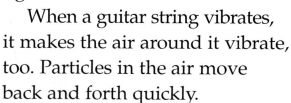

When someone plays a trumpet, air vibrates inside it. Touch the trumpet, and you can feel it vibrate.

The sound moves through the air. You hear the sound when the back-and-forth motion of the air reaches your ear.

If there was no air around you right now, would you hear anything? No. Sounds travel through air. Particles in the air vibrate. That's how air carries sounds.

You can also hear sounds underwater. Sounds travel through water and other liquids. Sounds can travel through solid objects, too. Put your ear on a desk. Tap the other end of the desk. You can hear the tapping noise through the desk.

Sounds can move through solids, liquids, and gases. Sounds move better through some kinds of matter, such as metals. Nonmetal materials, such as cotton, do not conduct sounds.

READING **Sequence of Events**
How do sounds from a guitar reach your ears?

Dolphins send sounds to each other through water.

FOR SCHOOL OR HOME

Paper Cup Phone

1. Make a hole in the bottom of a paper cup. Thread a string through the hole of the paper cup. Tie the end of the string to a paper clip. Tape the paper clip to the inside of the cup bottom.

2. Repeat step 1, tying a second paper cup to the other end of the string.

3. Experiment You have made a telephone. Find a partner. Speak softly into the cup, and have your partner listen. Switch roles. Record your observations.

4. Make a Hypothesis How well will your telephone work if you use a different type of string? Test your hypothesis.

5. Which string was better?

How Do Sounds Get Higher and Lower?

Tap the key at the far left of a piano keyboard. The sound is very deep, or low. Now move your finger along the keys to the right. The sound becomes higher and higher. You are changing the **pitch** (PICH) of the sound. A sound's pitch is how high or low it is.

What causes a change in pitch? Length is sometimes the answer. Shorter strings vibrate faster than longer ones. The faster a string vibrates, the higher the pitch of the sound.

Other times, thickness changes pitch. Thinner strings vibrate faster. Thinner strings have higher pitches.

Did you ever notice that guitars and pianos have screws on strings? Twist a screw, and the string becomes tighter. Tighter strings vibrate faster, making the pitch higher.

Notice the different lengths and thicknesses of the piano strings. Which string makes a higher pitch, 1 or 2?

▷ **What causes pitch to change?**

Pull the slide out. The air inside has a longer path. The pitch gets lower.

What Makes Sounds Loud or Soft?

Tap your desk. Then pound it harder. How has the sound changed? The pitch is the same. However, pounding the desk makes a louder sound than tapping it. **Volume** (VAHL·yewm) means how loud or soft a sound is.

Why do sounds have different volumes? Try whispering softly. Now call out loudly through a window. How did you make the different sounds? You had to take a deep breath to make the loud sound. You used more energy. Making loud sounds takes more energy than making soft sounds.

▷ **The sounds of a rocket launch are louder than the sounds kittens make. Why?**

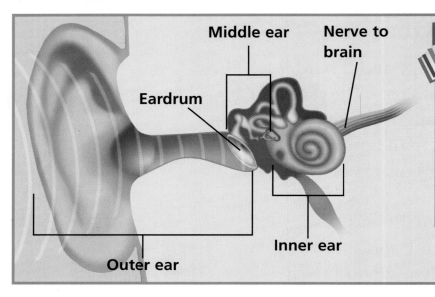

Middle ear

Nerve to brain

Eardrum

Inner ear

Outer ear

READING
Diagrams

1. What parts of the ear do sound vibrations pass through?

2. What part sends a signal to the brain?

How Do You Hear Sounds?

A sound takes less than a second to travel across a room to your ear. Then the sound must pass through your ear. A signal from the ear travels to the brain. This is how you hear sounds.

Never put a finger or pencil in your ear. You may damage the parts inside. Loud sounds can damage your ear as well. Loud sounds have a lot of energy. They can damage the way parts inside the ear vibrate. In time they can cause a loss of hearing.

▶ **What happens when sound reaches your ears?**

Hearing aids can help people who hear poorly. The hearing aid makes sounds louder.

Ground-crew workers must protect their ears.

L·I·N·K·S

Why It Matters

You depend on sounds in many ways. A buzzer sounds. It's time for school to begin. After school you listen to your favorite songs on the radio.

Animals use sounds, too. Sounds can warn animals of danger or help them find food. Many animals call to one another, just like humans do! Visit **www.mhscience02.com** to do a research project on sounds.

Think and Write

1. What do you need to do to make any sound?

2. Why can you hear sounds underwater?

3. How will the sound change when you loosen a guitar string?

4. Why might you cover your ears when a plane flies overhead?

5. **Critical Thinking** You hear nothing. Your dog jumps. Explain what happened.

MATH LINK

Make a chart. Volume is measured in units called decibels.

Kind of Sound	Decibels
Whisper	20
People talking	50
Heavy traffic	80
Thunder	110
Jet plane (30 meters away)	140

List sounds that you hear. Check to see if any of these sounds are shown on the chart above. Write down the decibel levels of these sounds. Then use research materials or the Internet to look up the remaining sounds on your list. Record this information in a chart.

WRITING LINK

Write a poem. Listen to the sounds around you. Write down how you hear the sounds. For example, you might hear a drip or a beep. Use these sound words to write a poem. Share your poem with your classmates.

TECHNOLOGY LINK

At the Computer Visit **www.mhscience02.com** for more links.

Paths for Electricity

Vocabulary

cell, F72

circuit, F72

electric current, F72

switch, F73

Get Ready

Have you ever played with an electric train set? The set has lots of parts. You need to put the parts together in the right way for the train to work. How do the parts need to be set up to make the train move?

Process Skill

You predict when you state possible results of an event or experiment.

F 70

Explore Activity

Materials
D-cell battery
small light bulb
20-cm wire

What Makes the Bulb Light?

Procedure

1. **Predict** Look at the bulb, wire, and battery. How might you put them together to make the bulb light? Record your ideas.

2. **Experiment** Try to light the bulb. Draw a picture of each setup that you try. Record which ones work and which ones don't.

Drawing Conclusions

1. How many ways did you find to light the bulb?

2. **Interpret Data** How were the ways that made the bulb light alike? How were they different from the ways that did not make the bulb light?

3. What is the job of the wire?

4. **Going Further: Predict** How could you light the bulb with two pieces of wire?

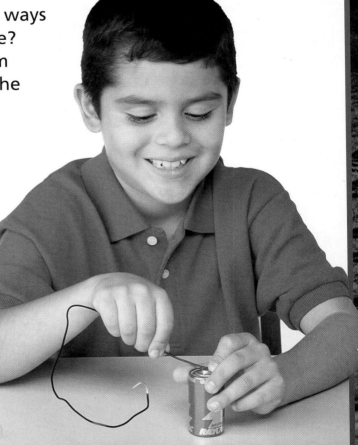

Main Idea Electricity is a form of energy. It travels in a path called a circuit.

What Makes a Bulb Light?

A **cell** (SEL) is a source of electricity. A battery is made up of two or more cells. With a bulb, wires, and a cell, you can use electricity to light the bulb. However, you need to put the parts together in the right way.

READING
Diagrams

Why is the second bulb unlit?

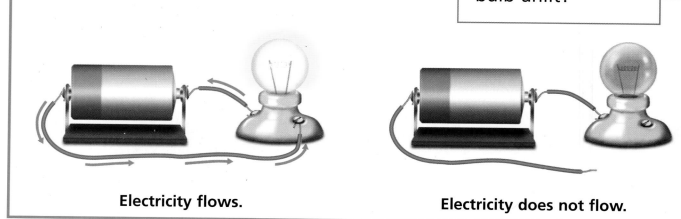

Electricity flows.   Electricity does not flow.

Electricity is a form of energy that travels in a **circuit** (SUR·kit). A circuit is a path in which electricity goes around and around. For the bulb to light, wires must connect it to the cell to form a circuit.

Electricity flowing through a circuit is called **electric current** (KUR·uhnt). Electric current can light a bulb, power a toy train, and do many other things!

These women are using cables to power a car battery. What part of the circuit are the cables?

How can you control the flow of electricity? One way is to use a **switch** (SWICH), such as the switch on a flashlight. A switch opens or closes an electric circuit.

When a flashlight switch is off, there is a gap in the circuit. The circuit is open. Electricity does not flow. Turn the switch on, and the gap is no longer there. The circuit is closed. Electricity flows, and the bulb lights.

Switches such as this one control the flow of electricity in your home.

READING **Sequence of Events**
What happens when you turn on a switch?

QUICK LAB

FOR SCHOOL OR HOME

Make a Flashlight

1. Use two D cells, a paper tube, 30 centimeters of wire, masking tape, and a flashlight bulb to make a model flashlight.

2. How does your model flashlight work?

3. Describe the electric circuit in the flashlight.

4. How does your model flashlight compare with a real flashlight?

5. Infer How might you improve your model?

How Do You Use Electricity?

How many ways do you use electricity at home? Almost everyone uses electric lights. You may also use electricity to heat your home. Electric machines include refrigerators, hair dryers, televisions, and vacuum cleaners.

▷ **What electric machines do you use?**

Electricity runs the motor in a vacuum cleaner.

Electricity is changed to microwaves. The microwaves cook the food.

Electricity changes to heat as it flows through coils in a toaster.

Electricity lights the tiny dots that make up the picture on a computer screen.

Lesson Review

Why It Matters

Electricity helps you do all sorts of things. Telephones use electricity to carry sound. You use electricity to cook your food and wash your clothes. You need electricity to run your computer and listen to the radio.

Think and Write

1. What is a cell?

2. What is a circuit?

3. How does a switch control the flow of electricity in a circuit?

4. Name four ways that you use electricity in your life.

5. **Critical Thinking** You turn the switch on a flashlight. The light does not come on! List three things that might be wrong with the flashlight.

L·I·N·K·S

MATH LINK

Solve a problem. Harvey has five flashlights. Each flashlight takes three D-cells. How many batteries does he need to power all five flashlights?

SOCIAL STUDIES LINK

Write a report. Years ago, people did not have electricity in their homes. Research how life was different without electricity. How did people cook food, stay cool in summer, or make light? Write down what you find out.

LITERATURE LINK

Read *Ben Franklin* to learn about the famous American inventor. When you finish reading the book, think about creating an invention of your own. Try the activities at the end of the book.

Ben Franklin

by Cynthia Benjamin

TECHNOLOGY LINK

Science Newsroom CD-ROM Choose *Let's Join the Circuits* to learn how circuits must be set up for electricity to flow through them.

At the Computer Visit **www.mhscience02.com** for more links.

Vocabulary

Fill in each blank with the best word from the list.

cell, F72   reflect, F55

heat, F42   refract, F56

insulator, F46   switch, F73

opaque, F54   vibrate, F64

pitch, F66   volume, F67

1. A form of energy that makes things warmer is _____.

2. A material that heat doesn't flow through easily is called a(n) _____.

3. An object that does not allow light to pass through it is _____.

4. Sound is made when an object _____.

5. A flashlight gets electricity from a(n) _____.

6. To open or close an electrical circuit, you use a(n) _____.

When light hits a surface, it can:

7. _____

8. _____.

Two properties of sound are:

9. _____

10. _____.

Test Prep

11. Heat can travel through _____.

   A solids

   B liquids

   C gases

   D all of the above

12. It is cold outside. You put on a warm jacket. The jacket is a(n) _____.

   F mixture

   G conductor

   H insulator

   J switch

13. Light travels _____.

   A in straight lines

   B in curvy lines

   C slowly

   D around objects

14. Objects that vibrate slowly make sounds with _____.

   F a high volume

   G no volume

   H a high pitch

   J a low pitch

15. Heat, light, sound, and electricity are all forms of _____.

A motion
B energy
C work
D friction

Concepts and Skills

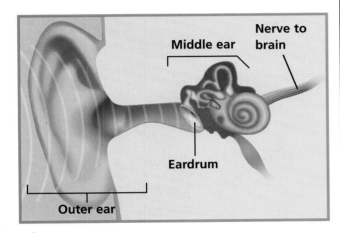

16. **Reading in Science** List the sentences in correct order. Use the diagram above to help you.
1. The middle ear vibrates.
2. A special nerve carries messages about sound to the brain.
3. A sound reaches your ear.

17. **Critical Thinking** How could you use mirrors and a light to signal your friend across the street? Write a short paragraph to describe your answer.

18. **Process Skills: Use Variables** Does salt water or fresh water freeze faster? Describe how you would test your ideas. What variable changes in the experiment?

19. **Scientific Methods** How could you find out if there is electrical energy in a cell? Write a hypothesis. Describe how you would test your idea.

20. **Safety** Imagine you are a safety officer. Are people in danger from very loud sounds in your community? Write some rules that would protect people from harmful noises.

Boost *your test scores!*

Be Smart!
Visit www.mhscience02.com to learn more.

Emmett Chappelle
Biochemist

Have you ever wondered who creates the new materials used to build the space shuttle? Or have you wondered who makes new medicines? If you have, you might want to become a chemist. A chemist makes new things by mixing two or more chemicals together.

Emmett Chappelle is a biochemist. A biochemist studies the chemicals in living things. He worked at NASA's Goddard Space Flight Center.

Early NASA spaceflights had a problem with the air inside spacecraft. The air became polluted with the same gas that comes out of cars. This gas is poisonous. Chappelle studied the problem. Green plants provided the answer. He discovered that small plants would take in the gas. Plants would keep the air clean and safe for the astronauts.

Today, Chappelle is still interested in plants. He is working with other scientists to help people grow better crops so there will be more food. They are doing very important research!

NASA's Goddard Space Flight Center in Maryland

Careers IN SCIENCE

Here is another career related to the study of chemistry. You can use the Internet or library resources to find out more about this career.

Forensic chemist

If you're interested in chemistry, you may want to be a forensic chemist. A forensic chemist is part chemist, part detective. After a crime has happened, evidence is collected. It is the job of the forensic scientist to test some of this evidence at a laboratory. The results of the tests help solve crimes. Sometimes they provide clues to help decide who did or did not commit the crime.

Write ABOUT IT

1. Describe the job of a chemist. What is one way chemists help people?

2. Chappelle discovered that plants aboard spacecraft would take in poisonous gases. How could this discovery help us fight air pollution on Earth?

AT THE COMPUTER

Visit www.mhscience02.com **to learn more about careers.**

A Question of BALANCE

What to Do

Find two objects that you think have the same mass. Cut three pieces of string that are 10 cm long. Use the string to tie each object to the ruler as shown. Tie the third piece of string to the center of the ruler. Hold the center string with your hand. Try to have the two sides balance. Try different objects until you are able to balance the ruler.

Draw Conclusions

Were you able to have the two sides of the ruler balance? Write a short paragraph to explain what happened.

SAND DANCE

Your goal is to make sand move without touching it.

What to Do

Stretch the plastic wrap over one end of the cardboard tube. Fasten it with the rubber band, as shown. Put a pinch of sand on the plastic wrap. Bring the tube near the radio. Turn the radio on. Watch what happens to the plastic wrap. Strike the tuning fork near the tube. Again, watch what happens to the plastic wrap.

Draw Conclusions

How did you make the sand move most? Which way of moving the sand produced the most sound energy? Explain why you think so.

For Your Reference

Science Handbook

Health Handbook

Glossary

Units of Measurement

Temperature

1. The temperature is 77 degrees Fahrenheit.

2. That is the same as 25 degrees Celsius.

3. Water boils at 212 degrees Fahrenheit.

4. Water freezes at 0 degrees Celsius.

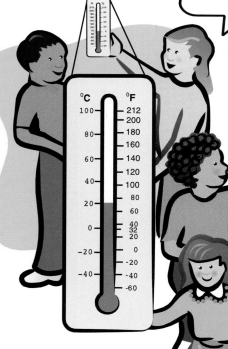

Length and Area

1. This classroom is 10 meters wide and 20 meters long.

2. That means the area is 200 square meters.

Mass and Weight

1. That baseball bat weighs 32 ounces.

2. 32 ounces is the same as 2 pounds.

3. The mass of the bat is 907 grams.

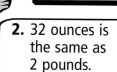

Measurement

Volume of Fluids

Weight/ Force

Rate

1. This bottle of juice has a volume of 1 liter.

2. That is a little more than 1 quart.

3. I weigh 85 pounds. That is a force of 380.8 newtons.

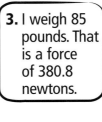

1. She can walk 20 meters in 5 seconds.

2. That means her speed is 4 meters per second.

Table of Measurements

SI (International System) of Units	English System of Units
Temperature Water freezes at 0 degrees Celsius (°C) and boils at 100°C.	**Temperature** Water freezes at 32 degrees Fahrenheit (°F) and boils at 212°F.
Length and Distance 10 millimeters (mm) = 1 centimeter (cm) 100 centimeters = 1 meter (m) 1,000 meters = 1 kilometer (km)	**Length and Distance** 12 inches (in.) = 1 foot (ft) 3 feet = 1 yard (yd) 5,280 feet = 1 mile (mi)
Volume 1 cubic centimeter (cm³) = 1 milliliter (mL) 1,000 milliliters = 1 liter (L)	**Volume of Fluids** 8 fluid ounces (fl oz) = 1 cup (c) 2 cups = 1 pint (pt) 2 pints = 1 quart (qt) 4 quarts = 1 gallon (gal)
Mass 1,000 milligrams (mg) = 1 gram (g) 1,000 grams = 1 kilogram (kg)	**Weight** 16 ounces (oz) = 1 pound (lb) 2,000 pounds = 1 ton (T)
Area 1 square kilometer (km²) =1 km x 1 km 1 hectare = 10,000 square meters (m²)	**Rate** mph = miles per hour
Rate m/s = meters per second km/h = kilometers per hour	
Force 1 newton (N) = 1 kg x 1m/s²	

Use a Hand Lens

You use a hand lens to magnify an object, or make the object look larger. With a hand lens, you can see details that would be hard to see without the hand lens.

Magnify a Piece of Cereal

1. Place a piece of your favorite cereal on a flat surface. Look at the cereal carefully. Draw a picture of it.

2. Hold the hand lens so that it is just above the cereal. Look through the lens, and slowly move it away from the cereal. The cereal will look larger.

3. Keep moving the hand lens until the cereal begins to look blurry. Then move the lens a little closer to the cereal until you can see it clearly.

4. Draw a picture of the cereal as you see it through the hand lens. Fill in details that you did not see before.

5. Repeat this activity using objects you are studying in science. It might be a rock, some soil, a seed, or something else.

Use a Microscope

Hand lenses make objects look several times larger. A microscope, however, can magnify an object to look hundreds of times larger.

Examine Salt Grains

1. Place the microscope on a flat surface. Always carry a microscope with both hands. Hold the arm with one hand, and put your other hand beneath the base.
2. Look at the drawing to learn the different parts of the microscope.
3. Move the mirror so that it reflects light up toward the stage. Never point the mirror directly at the Sun or a bright light. Bright light can cause permanent eye damage.
4. Place a few grains of salt on the slide. Put the slide under the stage clips on the stage. Be sure that the salt grains are over the hole in the stage.
5. Look through the eyepiece. Turn the focusing knob slowly until the salt grains come into focus.
6. Draw what the grains look like through the microscope.
7. Look at other objects through the microscope. Try a piece of leaf, a strand of human hair, or a pencil mark.
8. Draw what each object looks like through the microscope. Do any of the objects look alike? If so, how? Are any of the objects alive? How do you know?

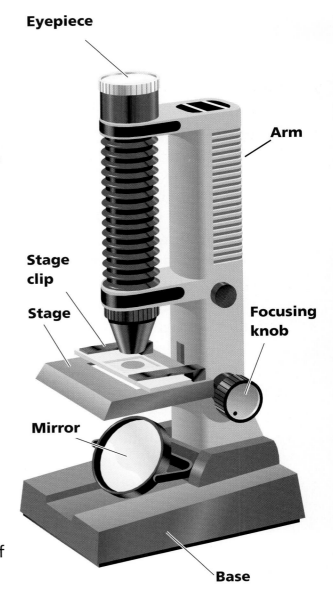

Eyepiece

Arm

Stage clip

Stage

Focusing knob

Mirror

Base

Measure Time

You use timing devices to measure how long something takes to happen. Some timing devices you use in science are a clock with a second hand and a stopwatch. Which one is more accurate?

Comparing a Clock and a Stopwatch

1. Look at a clock with a second hand. The second hand is the hand that you can see moving. It measures seconds.

2. Get an egg timer with falling sand. When the second hand of the clock points to 12, tell your partner to start the egg timer. Watch the clock while the sand in the egg timer is falling.

3. When the sand stops falling, count how many seconds it took. Record this measurement. Repeat the activity, and compare the two measurements.

4. Look at a stopwatch. Click the button on the top right. This starts the time. Click the button again. This stops the time. Click the button on the top left. This sets the stopwatch back to zero. Notice that the stopwatch tells time in hours, minutes, seconds, and hundredths of a second.

5. Repeat the activity in steps 1–3, but use the stopwatch instead of a clock. Make sure the stopwatch is set to zero. Click the top right button to start timing. Click the

button again when the sand stops falling. Make sure you and your partner time the sand twice.

0 minutes   **25 seconds 72 hundredths of a second**

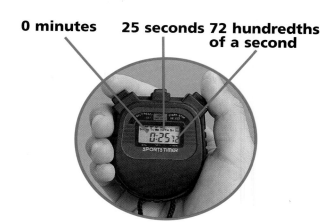

More About Time

1. Use the stopwatch to time how long it takes an ice cube to melt under cold running water. How long does an ice cube take to melt under warm running water?

2. Match each of these times with the action you think took that amount of time.

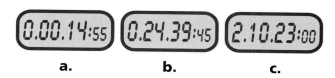

a.   b.   c.

1. A Little League baseball game
2. Saying the Pledge of Allegiance
3. Recess

Make Measurements

Measure Length

Find Length with a Ruler

1. Look at this section of a ruler. Each centimeter is divided into 10 millimeters. How long is the paper clip?

2. The length of the paper clip is 3 centimeters plus 2 millimeters. You can write this length as 3.2 centimeters.

3. Place a ruler on your desk. Lay a pencil against the ruler so that one end of the pencil lines up with the left edge of the ruler. Record the length of the pencil.

4. Trade pencils with a classmate. Measure and record the length of each other's pencils. Compare your answers.

Measuring Area

Area is the amount of surface something covers. To find the area of a rectangle, multiply the rectangle's length by its width. For example, the rectangle here is 3 centimeters long and 2 centimeters wide. Its area is 3 cm x 2 cm = 6 square centimeters. You write the area as 6 cm^2.

1. Find the area of your science book. Measure the book's length to the nearest centimeter. Measure its width.

2. Multiply the book's length by its width. Remember to put the answer in cm^2.

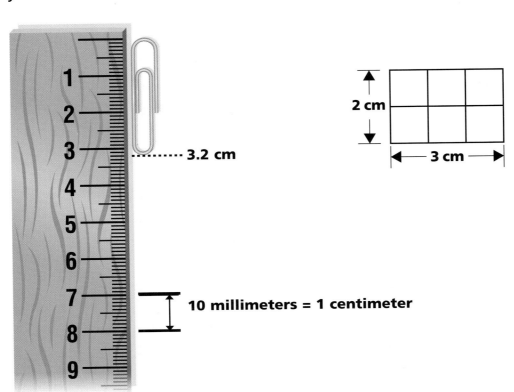

3.2 cm

2 cm

3 cm

10 millimeters = 1 centimeter

Measure Mass

Mass is the amount of matter an object has. You use a balance to measure mass. To find the mass of an object, you balance it with objects whose masses you know. Let's find the mass of a box of crayons.

Measure the Mass of a Box of Crayons

1. Place the balance on a flat, level surface.
2. Make sure the empty pans are balanced with each other. The pointer should point to the middle mark. If it does not, move the slider a little to the right or left to balance the pans.
3. Gently place a box of crayons on the left pan.
4. Add masses to the right pan until the pans are balanced.

5. Count the numbers on the masses that are in the right pan. The total is the mass of the box of crayons, in grams. Record this number. After the number, write a *g* for "grams."

More About Mass

What would happen if you replaced the crayons with a pineapple? You may not have enough masses to balance the pineapple. It has a mass of about 1,000 grams. That's the same as 1 kilogram, because *kilo* means "1,000."

Make Measurements

Measure Volume

Have you ever used a measuring cup? Measuring cups measure the volume of liquids. Volume is the amount of space something takes up. In science you use special measuring cups called beakers and graduated cylinders. These containers are marked in milliliters (mL).

Measure the Volume of a Liquid

1. Look at the beaker and at the graduated cylinder. The beaker has marks for each 25 mL up to 200 mL. The graduated cylinder has marks for each 1 mL up to 100 mL.

2. The surface of the water in the graduated cylinder curves up at the sides. You measure the volume by reading the height of the water at the flat part. What is the volume of water in the graduated cylinder? How much water is in the beaker?

3. Pour 50 mL of water from a pitcher into a graduated cylinder. The water should be at the 50-mL mark on the graduated cylinder. If you go over the mark, pour a little water back into the pitcher.

4. Pour the 50 mL of water into a beaker.

5. Repeat steps 3 and 4 using 30 mL, 45 mL, and 25 mL of water.

6. Measure the volume of water you have in the beaker. Do you have about the same amount of water as your classmates?

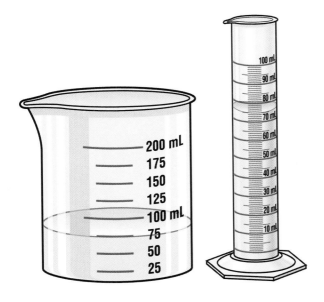

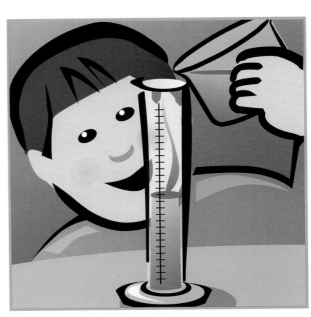

SCIENCE • HANDBOOK

R 9

Measure Weight/Force

You use a spring scale to measure weight. An object has weight because the force of gravity pulls down on the object. Therefore, weight is a force. Like all forces, weight is measured in newtons (N).

Measure the Weight of an Object

1. Look at your spring scale to see how many newtons it measures. See how the measurements are divided. The spring scale shown here measures up to 10 N. It has a mark for every 1 N.

2. Hold the spring scale by the top loop. Put the object to be measured on the bottom hook. If the object will not stay on the hook, place it in a net bag. Then hang the bag from the hook.

3. Let go of the object slowly. It will pull down on a spring inside the scale. The spring is connected to a pointer. The pointer on the spring scale shown here is a small arrow.

4. Wait for the pointer to stop moving. Read the number of newtons next to the pointer. This is the object's weight. The mug in the picture weighs 3 N.

More About Spring Scales

You probably weigh yourself by standing on a bathroom scale. This is a spring scale. The force of your body stretches a spring inside the scale. The dial on the scale is probably marked in pounds—the English unit of weight. One pound is equal to about 4.5 newtons.

Here are some spring scales you may have seen.

Measure Temperature

Temperature is how hot or cold something is. You use a thermometer to measure temperature. A thermometer is made of a thin tube with colored liquid inside. When the liquid gets warmer, it expands and moves up the tube. When the liquid gets cooler, it contracts and moves down the tube. You may have seen most temperatures measured in degrees Fahrenheit (°F). Scientists measure temperature in degrees Celsius (°C).

Read a Thermometer

1. Look at the thermometer shown here. It has two scales—a Fahrenheit scale and a Celsius scale. Every 20 degrees on each scale has a number.
2. What is the temperature shown on the thermometer? At what temperature does water freeze? Give your answers in °F and in °C.

How Is Temperature Measured?

1. Fill a large beaker about one-half full of cool water. Find the temperature of the water by holding a thermometer in the water. Do not let the bulb at the bottom of the thermometer touch the sides or bottom of the beaker.
2. Keep the thermometer in the water until the liquid in the tube stops moving— about a minute. Read and record the temperature on the Celsius scale.

3. Fill another large beaker one-half full of warm water from a faucet. Be careful not to burn yourself by using hot water.
4. Find and record the temperature of the warm water just as you did in steps 1 and 2.

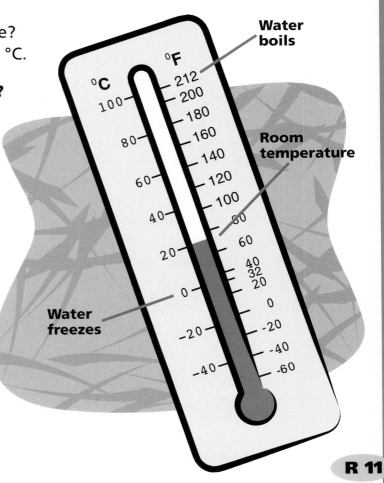

Water boils

°C

°F

Room temperature

Water freezes

Use Calculators: Add and Subtract

Sometimes after you make measurements, you have to add or subtract your numbers. A calculator helps you do this.

Add and Subtract Rainfall Amounts

The table shows the amount of rain that fell in a town each week during the summer.

Week	Rain (cm)
1	3
2	5
3	2
4	0
5	1
6	6
7	4
8	0
9	2
10	2
11	6
12	5

1. Make sure the calculator is on. Press the **ON** key.
2. To add the numbers, enter a number and press **+** . Repeat until you enter the last number. Then press **=** . You do not have to enter the zeros. Your total should be 36.

3. What if you found out that you made a mistake in your measurement? Week 1 should be 2 cm less, week 6 should be 3 cm less, week 11 should be 1 cm less, and week 12 should be 2 cm less. Subtract these numbers from your total. You should have 36 displayed on the calculator. Press **−** , and enter the first number you want to subtract. Repeat until you enter the last number. Then press **=** .

Use Calculators: Multiply and Divide

Sometimes after you make measurements, you have to multiply or divide your measurements to get other information. A calculator helps you multiply and divide, especially if the numbers have decimal points.

Multiply Decimals

What if you are measuring the width of your classroom? You discover that the floor is covered with tiles and the room is exactly 32 tiles wide. You measure a tile, and it is 22.7 centimeters wide. To find the width of the room, you can multiply 32 by 22.7.

1. Make sure the calculator is on. Press the **ON** key.
2. Press **3** and **2**.
3. Press **×**.
4. Press **2**, **2**, **.**, and **7**.
5. Press **=**. Your total should be 726.4. That is how wide the room is in centimeters.

Divide Decimals

Now what if you wanted to find out how many desks placed side by side would be needed to reach across the room? You measure one desk, and it is 60 centimeters wide. To find the number of desks needed, divide 726.4 by 60.

1. Turn the calculator on.
2. Press **7**, **2**, **6**, **.**, and **4**.
3. Press **÷**.
4. Press **6** and **0**.
5. Press **=**. Your total should be about 12.1. This means you can fit 12 desks across the room with a little space left over.

What if the room was 35 tiles wide? How wide would the room be? How many desks would fit across it?

Use Computers

A computer has many uses. The Internet connects your computer to many other computers around the world, so you can collect all kinds of information. You can use a computer to show this information and write reports. Best of all, you can use a computer to explore, discover, and learn.

You can also get information from CD-ROMs. They are computer disks that can hold large amounts of information. You can fit a whole encyclopedia on one CD-ROM.

Use Computers for a Project

Here is how one group of students uses computers as they work on a weather project.

1. The students use instruments to measure temperature, wind speed, wind direction, and other parts of the weather. They input this information, or data, into the computer. The students keep the data in a table. This helps them compare the data from one day to the next.

2. The teacher finds out that another group of students in a town 200 kilometers to the west is also doing a weather project. The two groups use the Internet to talk to each other and share data. When a storm happens in the town to the west, that group tells the other group that it's coming its way.

Use Technology

email: It's going to storm here. The sky is turning dark gray. The winds are sometimes 65 km per hour from the northwest.

3. The students want to find out more. They decide to stay on the Internet and send questions to a local TV weather forecaster. She has a website and answers questions from students every day.

4. Meanwhile some students go to the library to gather more information from a CD-ROM disk. The CD-ROM has an encyclopedia that includes movie clips with sound. The clips give examples of different kinds of storms.

5. The students have kept all their information in a folder called Weather Project. Now they use that information to write a report about the weather. On the computer they can move paragraphs, add words, take out words, put in diagrams, and draw their own weather maps. Then they print the report in color.

6. Use the information on these two pages to plan your own investigation. Use a computer, the Internet, a CD-ROM, or any other technological device.

Make Graphs to Organize Data

When you do an experiment in science, you collect information. To find out what your information means, you can organize it into graphs. There are many kinds of graphs.

Bar Graphs

A bar graph uses bars to show information. For example, what if you are growing a plant? Every week you measure how high the plant has grown. Here is what you find.

Week	Height (cm)
1	1
2	3
3	6
4	10
5	17
6	20
7	22
8	23

The bar graph at right organizes the measurements you collected so that you can easily compare them.

1. Look at the bar for week 2. Put your finger at the top of the bar. Move your finger straight over to the left to find how many centimeters the plant grew by the end of week 2.

2. Between which two weeks did the plant grow most?

3. When did plant growth begin to level off?

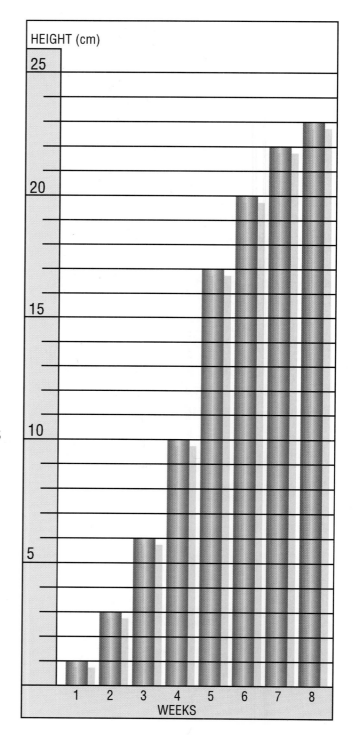

Represent Data

Pictographs

A pictograph uses symbols, or pictures, to show information. What if you collect information about how much water your family uses each day? Here is what you find.

Activity	Water Used Each Day (L)
Drinking	10
Showering	100
Bathing	120
Brushing teeth	40
Washing dishes	80
Washing hands	30
Washing clothes	160
Flushing toilet	50

You can organize this information into the pictograph shown here. In this pictograph each bottle means 20 liters of water. A half bottle means half of 20, or 10 liters of water.

1. Which activity uses the most water?
2. Which activity uses the least water?

Line Graphs

A line graph shows information by connecting dots plotted on the graph. It shows change over time. What if you measure the temperature outdoors every hour starting at 6 A.M.? Here is what you find.

Time	Temperature (°C)
6 A.M.	10
7 A.M.	12
8 A.M.	14
9 A.M.	16
10 A.M.	18
11 A.M.	20

You can organize this information into a line graph. Follow these steps.

1. Make a scale along the bottom and side of the graph. The scales should include all the numbers in the chart. Label the scales.
2. Plot points on the graph.
3. Connect the points with a line.

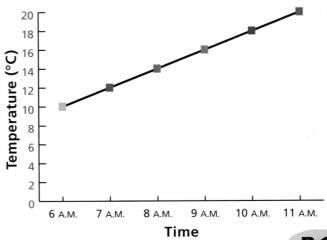

Represent Data

Make Maps, Tables, Charts

Locate Places

A map is a drawing that shows an area from above. Most maps have numbers and letters along the top and side. What if you wanted to find the library on the map below? It is located at D7. Place a finger on the letter D along the side of the map and another finger on the number 7 at the top. Then move your fingers straight across and down the map until they meet. The library is located where D and 7 meet.

1. What building is located at G3?
2. The hospital is located three blocks south and three blocks east of the library. What is its number and letter?
3. Make a map of an area in your community. It might be a park or the area between your home and school. Include numbers and letters along the top and side. Use a compass to find north, and mark north on your map. Exchange maps with classmates.

Idea Maps

The map below left shows how places are connected to each other. Idea maps, on the other hand, show how ideas are connected to each other. Idea maps help you organize information about a topic.

Look at the idea map below. It connects ideas about water. This map shows that Earth's water is either fresh water or salt water. The map also shows four sources of fresh water. You can see that there is no connection between "rivers" and "salt water" on the map. This reminds you that salt water does not flow in rivers.

Make an idea map about a topic you are learning in science. Your map can include words, phrases, or even sentences. Arrange your map in a way that makes sense to you and helps you understand the ideas.

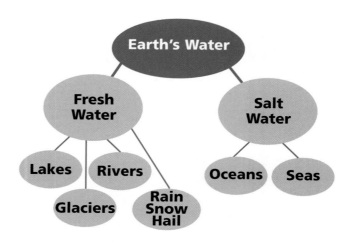

Make Tables and Charts to Organize Data

Tables help to organize data during experiments. Most tables have columns that run up and down, and rows that run across. The columns and rows have headings that tell you what kind of data goes in each part of the table.

A Sample Table

What if you are going to do an experiment to find out how long different kinds of seeds take to sprout? Before you begin the experiment, you should set up your table. Follow these steps.

1. In this experiment you will plant 20 radish seeds, 20 bean seeds, and 20 corn seeds. Your table must show how many of each kind of seed sprouted on days 1, 2, 3, 4, and 5.

2. Make your table with columns, rows, and headings. You might use a computer. Some computer programs let you build a table with just the click of a mouse. You can delete or add columns and rows if you need to.

3. Give your table a title. Your table could look like the one here.

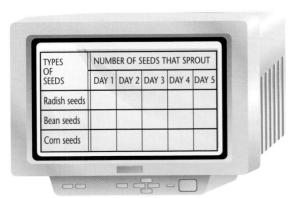

TYPES OF SEEDS	NUMBER OF SEEDS THAT SPROUT				
	DAY 1	DAY 2	DAY 3	DAY 4	DAY 5
Radish seeds					
Bean seeds					
Corn seeds					

Make a Table

Plant 20 bean seeds in each of two trays. Keep each tray at a different temperature, as shown above, and observe the trays for seven days. Make a table that you can use for this experiment. You can use the table to record, examine, and evaluate the information of this experiment.

Make a Chart

A chart is simply a table with pictures, as well as words to label the rows or columns. Make a chart that shows the information of the above experiment.

The Skeletal System

The body has a supporting frame, called a skeleton, which is made up of bones. The skeleton has several jobs.

- It gives the body its shape.
- It protects organs in the body.
- It works with muscles to move the body.

Each of the 206 bones of the skeleton is the size and shape best fitted to do its job. For example, long and strong leg bones support the body's weight.

The Skeleton

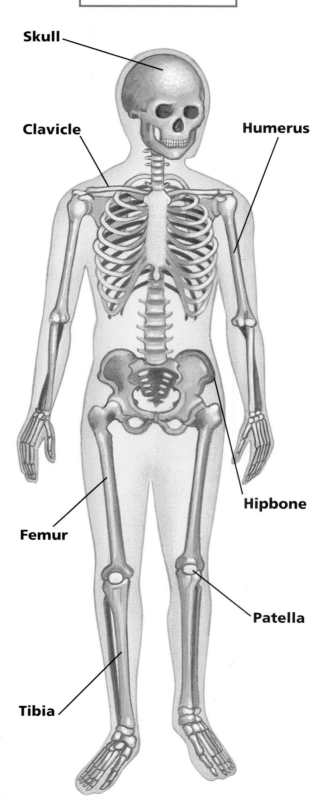

Skull

Clavicle

Humerus

Femur

Hipbone

Patella

Tibia

CARE!

- Exercise to keep your skeletal system in good shape.
- Don't overextend your joints.

Bones

1 A bone is covered with a tough but thin membrane that has many small blood vessels. The blood vessels bring nutrients and oxygen to the living parts of the bone and remove wastes.

2 Inside some bones is a soft tissue known as marrow. Yellow marrow is made mostly of fat cells and is one of the body's energy reserves. It is usually found in the long, hollow spaces of long bones.

3 Part of the bone is compact, or solid. It is made up of living bone cells and non-living materials. The nonliving part is made up of layers of hardened minerals such as calcium and phosphorus. In between the mineral layers are living bone cells.

4 Red marrow fills the spaces in spongy bone. Red marrow makes new red blood cells, germ-fighting white blood cells, and cell fragments that stop a cut from bleeding.

5 Part of the bone is made of bone tissue that looks like a dry sponge. It is made of strong, hard tubes. It is also found in the middle of short, flat bones.

CARE!

- **Eat foods rich in vitamins and minerals. Your bones need the minerals calcium and phosphorus to grow strong.**
- **Be careful! Avoid sprains and fractures.**
- **Get help in case of injury.**

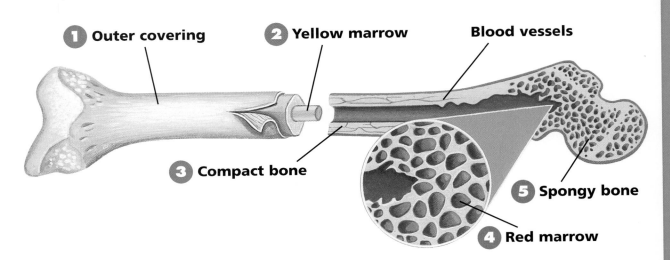

1 Outer covering   **2 Yellow marrow**   **Blood vessels**

3 Compact bone   **5 Spongy bone**   **4 Red marrow**

Joints

The skeleton has different types of joints. A joint is a place where two or more bones meet. Joints can be classified into three major groups—immovable joints, partly movable joints, and movable joints.

Types of Joints

IMMOVABLE JOINTS

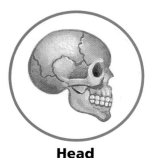

Head

Immovable joints are places where bones fit together too tightly to move. Nearly all the 29 bones in the skull meet at immovable joints. Only the lower jaw can move.

PARTLY MOVABLE JOINTS

Partly movable joints are places where bones can move only a little. Ribs are connected to the breastbone with these joints.

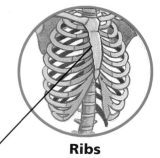

Breastbone

Ribs

MOVABLE JOINTS

Movable joints are places where bones can move easily.

Gliding joint

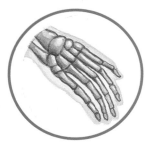

Hand and wrist

Small bones in the wrists and ankles meet at gliding joints. The bones can slide against one another. These joints allow some movement in all directions.

The hips are examples of ball-and-socket joints. The ball of one bone fits into the socket, or cup, of another bone. These joints allow bones to move back and forth, in a circle, and side to side.

Ball-and-socket joint

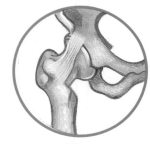

Hip

Hinge joint

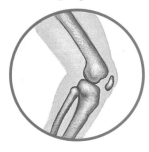

Knee

The knees are hinge joints. A hinge joint is similar to a door hinge. It allows bones to move back and forth in one direction.

The joint between the skull and neck is a pivot joint. It allows the head to move up and down, and side to side.

Pivot joint

Neck

The Muscular System

1 A message from your brain causes this muscle, called the biceps, to contract. When a muscle contracts, it becomes shorter and thicker. As the biceps contracts, it pulls on the arm bone it is attached to.

2 Most muscles work in pairs to move bones. This muscle, called the triceps, relaxes when the biceps contracts. When a muscle relaxes, it becomes longer and thinner.

3 To straighten your arm, a message from your brain causes the triceps to contract. When the triceps contracts, it pulls on the bone it is attached to.

4 As the triceps contracts, the biceps relaxes. Your arm straightens.

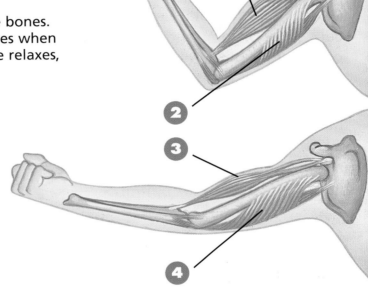

Three types of muscles make up the body—skeletal muscle, cardiac muscle, and smooth muscle.

The muscles that are attached to and move bones are called skeletal muscles. These muscles are attached to bones by a tough cord called a tendon. Skeletal muscles pull bones to move them. Muscles do not push bones.

Cardiac muscles are found in only one place in the body—the heart. The walls of the heart are made of strong cardiac muscles. When cardiac muscles contract, they squeeze blood out of the heart. When cardiac muscles relax, the heart fills with more blood.

Smooth muscles make up internal organs and blood vessels. Smooth muscles in the lungs help a person breathe. Those in the blood vessels help control blood flow around the body.

CARE!

- **Exercise to strengthen your muscles.**
- **Eat the right foods.**
- **Get plenty of rest.**

The Circulatory System

The circulatory system consists of the heart, blood vessels, and blood. Circulation is the flow of blood through the body. Blood is a liquid that contains red blood cells, white blood cells, and platelets. Red blood cells carry oxygen and nutrients to cells. White blood cells work to fight germs that enter the body. Platelets are cell fragments that make the blood clot.

The heart is a muscular organ about the size of a fist. It beats about 70 to 90 times a minute, pumping blood through the blood vessels. Arteries carry blood away from the heart. Some arteries carry blood to the lungs, where the cells pick up oxygen. Other arteries carry oxygen-rich blood from the lungs to all other parts of the body. Veins carry blood from other parts of the body back to the heart. Blood in most veins carries the wastes released by cells and has little oxygen. Blood flows from arteries to veins through narrow vessels called capillaries.

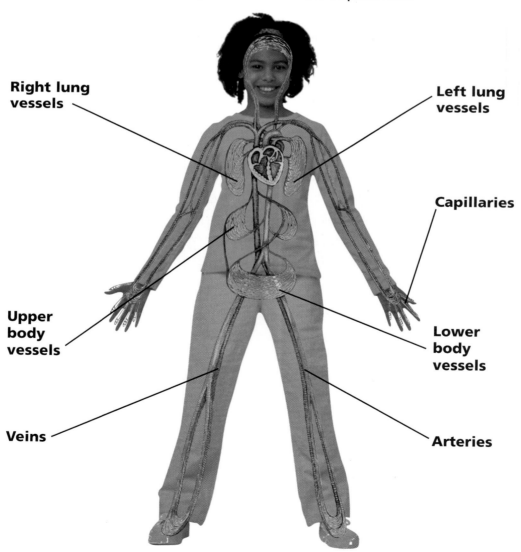

Right lung vessels

Left lung vessels

Capillaries

Upper body vessels

Lower body vessels

Veins

Arteries

The Heart

The heart has two sides, right and left, separated by a thick muscular wall. Each side has two chambers for blood. The upper chamber is the atrium. The lower chamber is the ventricle. Blood enters the heart through the vena cava. It leaves the heart through the aorta.

The pulmonary artery carries blood from the body into the lungs. Here carbon dioxide leaves the blood to be exhaled by the lungs. Fresh oxygen enters the blood to be carried to every cell in the body. Blood returns from the lungs to the heart through the pulmonary veins.

CARE!

- Don't smoke. The nicotine in tobacco makes the heart beat faster and work harder to pump blood.

- Never take illegal drugs, such as cocaine or heroin. They can damage the heart and cause heart failure.

To the Lungs

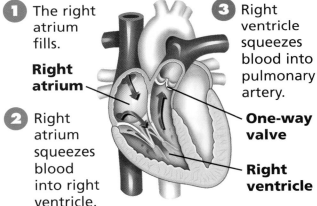

1 The right atrium fills.

Right atrium

2 Right atrium squeezes blood into right ventricle.

3 Right ventricle squeezes blood into pulmonary artery.

One-way valve

Right ventricle

How the Heart Works

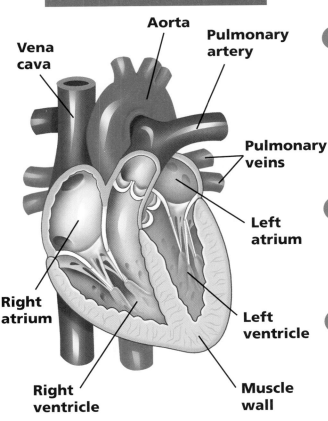

Vena cava

Aorta

Pulmonary artery

Pulmonary veins

Left atrium

Right atrium

Left ventricle

Right ventricle

Muscle wall

From the Lungs

1 The left atrium fills.

2 Left atrium squeezes blood into left ventricle.

3 Left ventricle squeezes blood into aorta.

Left atrium

One-way valve

Left ventricle

The Respiratory System

The process of getting and using oxygen in the body is called respiration. When a person inhales, air is pulled into the nose or mouth. The air travels down into the trachea. In the chest the trachea divides into two bronchial tubes. One bronchial tube enters each lung. Each bronchial tube branches into smaller tubes called bronchioles.

At the end of each bronchiole are tiny air sacs called alveoli. The alveoli exchange carbon dioxide for oxygen.

Oxygen comes from the air we breathe. Two muscles control breathing, the lungs and a dome-shaped sheet of muscle called the diaphragm.

To inhale, the diaphragm contracts and pulls down. To exhale, the diaphragm relaxes and returns to its dome shape.

CARE!

- **Don't smoke. Smoking damages your respiratory system.**

- **Exercise to strengthen your breathing muscles.**

- **If you ever have trouble breathing, tell an adult at once.**

Air Flow

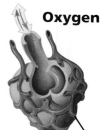

Carbon dioxide   **Oxygen**

Carbon dioxide diffuses into the alveoli. From there it is exhaled.

Capillary net

Alveoli

Fresh oxygen diffuses from the alveoli to the blood.

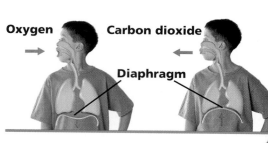

Oxygen   Carbon dioxide

Diaphragm

The air you breathe is about 21 percent oxygen.

The blood in the capillaries of your lungs has very little oxygen.

The blood has a higher concentration of carbon dioxide than air.

Throat

Trachea

Lungs

Activity Pyramid

Physical fitness is the condition in which the body is healthy and works the best it can. It involves working the skeletal muscles, bones, joints, heart, and respiratory system.

3–5 times a week
Aerobic activities such as swimming, biking, climbing; sports activities such as basketball, handball

Occasionally
Inactive pastimes such as watching TV, playing board games, talking on the phone

2–3 times a week
Leisure activities such as gardening, golf, softball

The activity pyramid shows you the kinds of exercises and other activities you should be doing to make your body more physically fit.

Daily Substitute activity for inactivity— take the stairs, walk instead of riding, bike instead of taking the bus

Food Guide Pyramid

To make sure the body stays fit and healthy, a person needs to eat a balanced diet. The Food Guide Pyramid shows how many servings of each group a person should eat every day.

CARE!

- **Stay active every day.**
- **Eat a balanced diet.**
- **Drink plenty of water— 6 to 8 large glasses a day.**

Fats, oils, and sweets
Use sparingly

Milk, yogurt, and cheese group
2–3 servings

Meat, dry beans, eggs, and nuts group
2–3 servings

Vegetable group
3–5 servings

Fruit group
2–4 servings

Bread, cereal, rice, and pasta group
6–11 servings

The Digestive System

Digestion is the process of breaking down food into simple substances the body can use. Digestion begins when a person chews food. Chewing breaks the food down into smaller pieces and moistens it with saliva. Saliva is produced by the salivary glands.

Digested food is absorbed in the small intestine. The walls of the small intestine are lined with villi. Villi are tiny fingerlike projections that absorb digested food. From the villi the blood transports nutrients to every part of the body.

CARE!

- Chew your food well.
- Drink plenty of water to help move food through your digestive system.

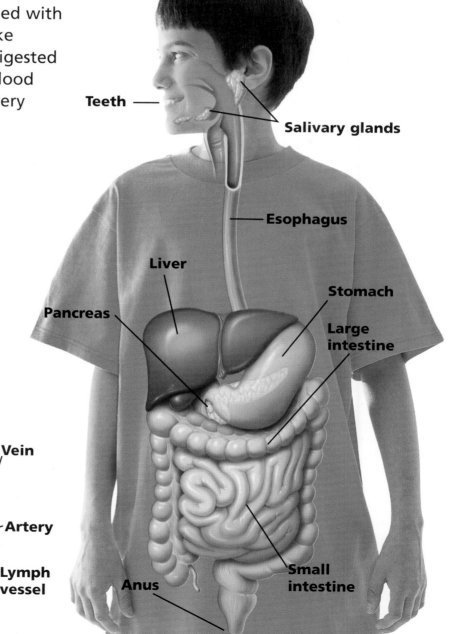

Capillary

Villi

Vein

Artery

Lymph vessel

Teeth

Salivary glands

Esophagus

Liver

Pancreas

Stomach

Large intestine

Small intestine

Anus

The Excretory System

Excretion is the process of removing waste products from the body. The liver filters wastes from the blood and converts them into urea. Urea is then carried to the kidneys for excretion.

The skin takes part in excretion when a person sweats. Glands in the inner layer of the skin produce sweat. Sweat is mostly water. Sweat tastes salty because it contains mineral salts the body doesn't need. There is also a tiny amount of urea in sweat.

Sweat is excreted onto the outer layer of the skin. Evaporation into the air takes place in part because of body heat. When sweat evaporates, a person feels cooler.

How You Sweat

Glands under your skin push sweat up to the surface, where it collects.

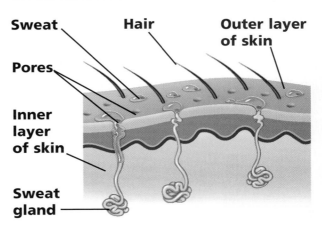

Sweat · Hair · Outer layer of skin · Pores · Inner layer of skin · Sweat gland

CARE!

- **Wash regularly to avoid body odor, clogged pores, and skin irritation.**

How Your Kidneys Work

1. Blood enters the kidney through an artery and flows into capillaries.

2. Sugars, salts, water, urea, and other wastes move from the capillaries to tiny nephrons.

3. Nutrients return to the blood and flow back out through veins.

4. Urea and other wastes become urine, which flows down the ureters.

5. Urine is stored in the bladder and excreted through the urethra.

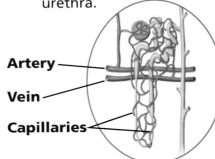

Artery · Vein · Capillaries

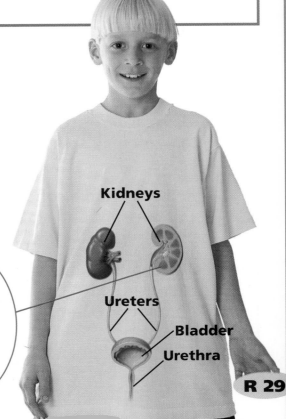

Kidneys · Ureters · Bladder · Urethra

The Nervous System

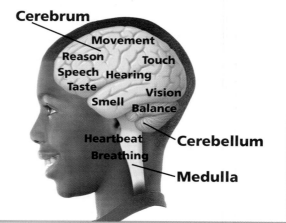

Cerebrum
Movement
Reason
Touch
Speech Hearing
Taste
Vision
Smell
Balance
Heartbeat
Breathing
Cerebellum
Medulla

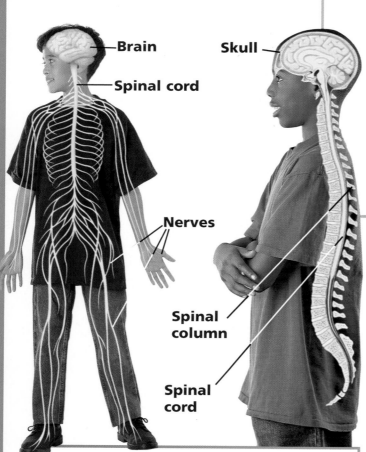

Brain

Spinal cord

Skull

Nerves

Spinal column

Spinal cord

CARE!

- To protect the brain and spinal cord, wear protective headgear when you play sports or exercise.

- Stay away from alcohol, which is a depressant and slows down the nervous system.

- Stay away from drugs, such as stimulants, which can speed up the nervous system.

The nervous system has two parts. The brain and the spinal cord are the central nervous system. All other nerves are the outer nervous system.

The largest part of the brain is the cerebrum. A deep groove separates the right half, or hemisphere, of the cerebrum from the left half. Both sides of the cerebrum contain control centers for the senses.

The cerebellum lies below the cerebrum. It coordinates the skeletal muscles. It also helps in keeping balance.

The brain stem connects to the spinal cord. The lowest part of the brain stem is the medulla. It controls heartbeat, breathing, blood pressure, and the muscles in the digestive system.

The Endocrine System

Hormones are chemicals that control body functions. A gland that produces hormones is called an endocrine gland. Sweat from sweat glands flows out of tubes called ducts. Endocrine glands have no ducts.

The endocrine glands are scattered around the body. Each gland makes one or more hormones. Every hormone seeks out a target organ. This is the place in the body where the hormone acts.

Some Glands in the Endocrine System

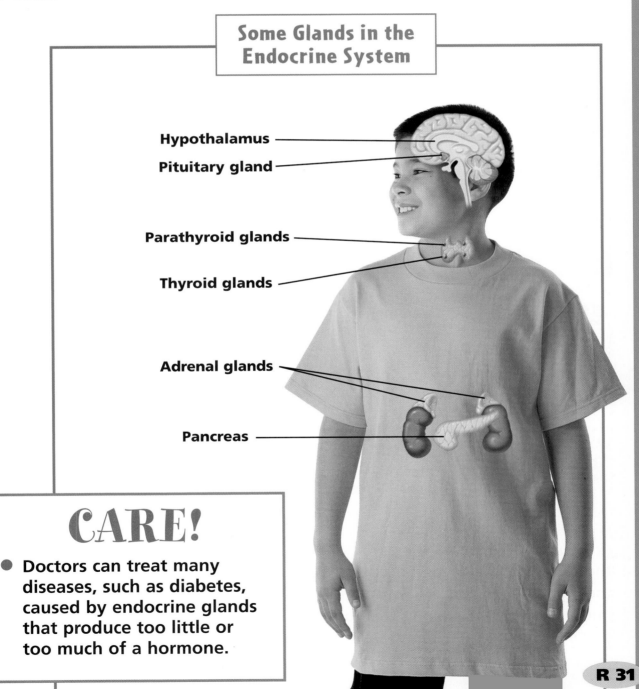

- Hypothalamus
- Pituitary gland
- Parathyroid glands
- Thyroid glands
- Adrenal glands
- Pancreas

CARE!

- Doctors can treat many diseases, such as diabetes, caused by endocrine glands that produce too little or too much of a hormone.

The Senses

Seeing

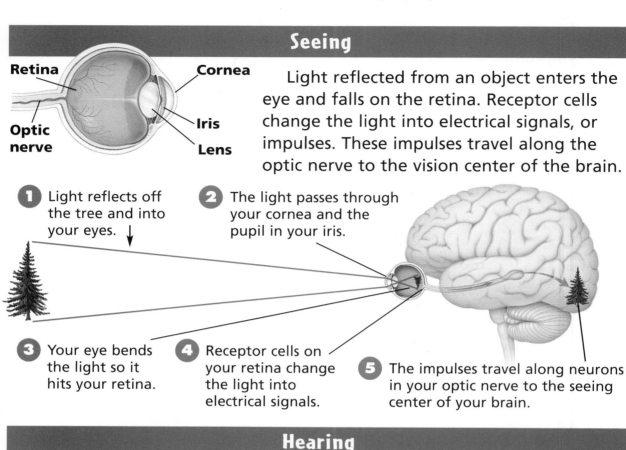

Retina
Optic nerve
Cornea
Iris
Lens

Light reflected from an object enters the eye and falls on the retina. Receptor cells change the light into electrical signals, or impulses. These impulses travel along the optic nerve to the vision center of the brain.

1 Light reflects off the tree and into your eyes.

2 The light passes through your cornea and the pupil in your iris.

3 Your eye bends the light so it hits your retina.

4 Receptor cells on your retina change the light into electrical signals.

5 The impulses travel along neurons in your optic nerve to the seeing center of your brain.

Hearing

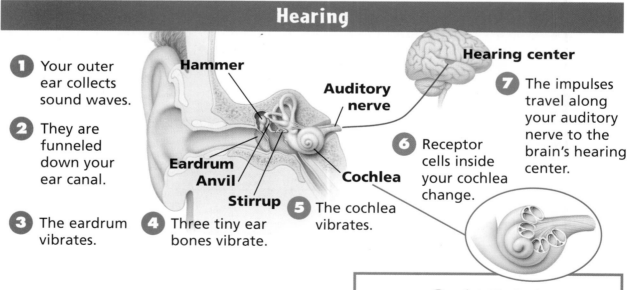

Hammer
Auditory nerve
Hearing center
Eardrum
Anvil
Stirrup
Cochlea

1 Your outer ear collects sound waves.

2 They are funneled down your ear canal.

3 The eardrum vibrates.

4 Three tiny ear bones vibrate.

5 The cochlea vibrates.

6 Receptor cells inside your cochlea change.

7 The impulses travel along your auditory nerve to the brain's hearing center.

Sound waves enter the ear and cause the eardrum to vibrate. Receptor cells in the ear change the sound waves into impulses that travel along the auditory nerve to the hearing center of the brain.

CARE!

- Avoid loud music.
- Don't sit too close to the TV screen.

The Senses

Smelling

The sense of smell is really the ability to detect chemicals in the air. When a person breathes, chemicals dissolve in mucus in the upper part of the nose. When the chemicals come in contact with receptor cells, the cells send impulses along the olfactory nerve to the smelling center of the brain.

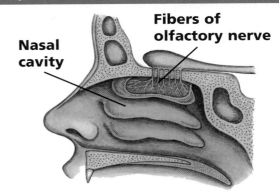

Nasal cavity

Fibers of olfactory nerve

Tasting

When a person eats, chemicals in food dissolve in saliva. Inside each taste bud are receptors that can sense the four main tastes—sweet, sour, salty, and bitter. The receptors send impulses along a nerve to the taste center of the brain. The brain identifies the taste of the food.

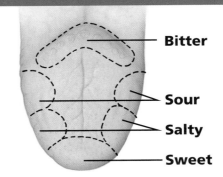

Bitter

Sour

Salty

Sweet

Touching

Receptor cells in the skin help a person tell hot from cold, wet from dry, and the light touch of a feather from the pressure of stepping on a stone. Each receptor cell sends impulses along sensory nerves to the spinal cord. The spinal cord then sends the impulses to the touch center of the brain.

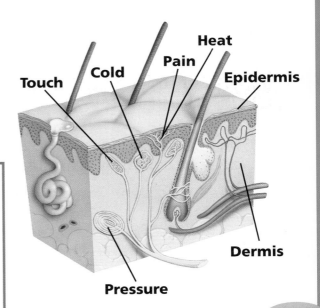

Touch   Cold   Pain   Heat   Epidermis

Dermis

Pressure

CARE!

- To prevent the spread of germs, always cover your mouth and nose when you cough or sneeze.

The Immune System

The immune system helps the body fight disease. When a person has a cut, germ-fighting white blood cells rush to the wound. There are white blood cells in the blood vessels and in the lymph vessels. Lymph vessels are similar to blood vessels. Instead of blood, they carry lymph. Lymph is a straw-colored fluid surrounding body cells.

Lymph nodes filter out harmful materials in the body. They also produce white blood cells to fight infections. Swollen lymph nodes in the neck are a clue that the body is fighting germs.

Lymph vessels run through your body to collect fluid and return it to the bloodstream.

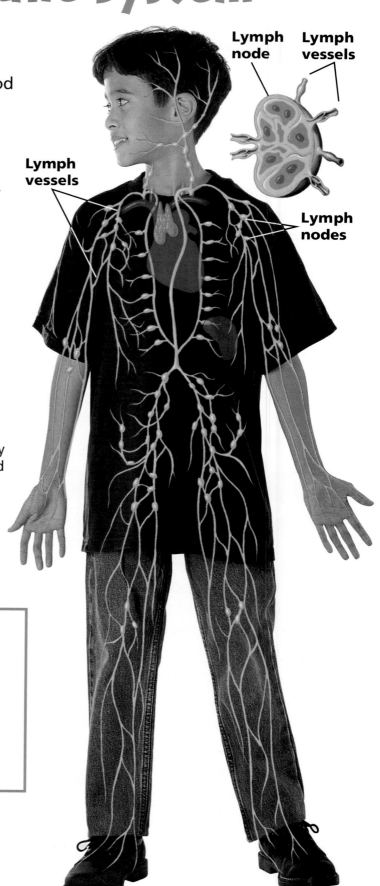

Lymph node

Lymph vessels

Lymph vessels

Lymph nodes

CARE!

● **Be sure to get immunized against common diseases.**

● **Keep cuts clean to prevent infection.**

Glossary

This Glossary will help you to pronounce and understand the meanings of the Science Words introduced in this book. The page number at the end of the definition tells where the word appears.

A

adaptation (ad'əp tā'shən) A special characteristic that helps an organism survive. (p. B50)

air (âr) A mixture of gases and dust. (p. D6)

air pressure (âr presh'ər) The force of air pushing down on Earth. (p. D9)

algae (al'jē) *pl. n., sing.* (-gə) Tiny one-celled organisms. (pp. B9, B27)

amber (am'bər) Hardened tree sap, often a source of insect fossils. (p. C22)

amphibian (am fib'ē ən) An animal that spends part of its life in water and part of its life on land. (p. A72)

anemometer (an'ə mom'i tər) A device that measures wind speed. (p. D25)

aqueduct (ak'wə dukt') A pipe or channel for carrying water over long distances. (p. C32)

atmosphere (at'məs fîr') Gases that surround Earth. (p. D6)

atom (at'əm) The smallest particle of matter. (p. F28)

axis (ak'sis) A real or imaginary line through the center of a spinning object. (p. D37)

PRONUNCIATION KEY

The following symbols are used throughout the McGraw-Hill Science 2002 Glossaries.

a at	e end	o hot	u up	hw white	ə about
ā ape	ē me	ō old	ū use	ng song	taken
ä far	i it	ôr fork	ü rule	th thin	pencil
âr care	ī ice	oi oil	u̇ pull	th this	lemon
ô law	îr pierce	ou out	ûr turn	zh measure	circus

' = primary accent; shows which syllable takes the main stress, such as **kil** in **kilogram** (kil'ə gram').
' = secondary accent; shows which syllables take lighter stresses, such as **gram** in **kilogram**.

B

bacteria, (bak tîr′ē ə) One-celled living things. (p. B18)

barometer (bə rom′i tər) A device for measuring air pressure. (p. D24)

bird (bûrd) An animal that has a beak, feathers, two wings, and two legs. (p. A73)

bulb (bulb) The underground stem of such plants as onions and irises. (p. A30)

C

camouflage (kam′ə fläzh) An adaptation that allows animals to blend into their surroundings. (p. B52)

carbon dioxide and oxygen cycles (kär′bən dī ok′sīd and ok′sə jən sī′kəlz) The process of passing oxygen and carbon dioxide from one population to another in both water and land habitats. (p. B27)

carnivore (kär′nə vôr′) An animal that eats only other animals. (p. B20)

cast (kast) A fossil formed or shaped inside a mold. (p. C23)

cell (sel) **1.** The basic building block of life. (p. A10) **2.** A source of electricity. (p. F72)

cell membrane (sel mem′brān′) The thin outer covering of a cell. (p. A10)

cell wall (sel wôl) A stiff layer outside the cell membrane of plant cells. (p. A11)

chemical change (kəm′i kəl chānj) A change that forms a different kind of matter. (p. F30)

chloroplast (klôr′ə plast′) One of the small green bodies inside a plant cell that makes foods for the plant. (p. A11)

circuit (sûr′kit) The path electricity flows through. (p. F72)

classify (klas′ə fī) To place materials that share properties together in groups. (p. S7)

communicate (kə mü′ni kāt′) To share information. (p. S7)

community (kə mü′ni tē) All the living things in an ecosystem. (p. B6)

competition (kom′pi tish′ən) The struggle among organisms for water, food, or other needs. (p. B42)

compound (kom′pound) Two or more elements put together. (p. F30)

compound machine (kom′pound mə shēn′) Two or more simple machines put together. (p. E57)

condense (kən dens′) *v.* To change from a gas to a liquid. (pp. C31, F17) —**condensation** (kon′den sā′shən) *n.* (p. D17)

conductor (kən duk′tər) A material that heat travels through easily. (p. F46)

conifer (kon′ə fər) A tree that produces seeds inside of cones. (p. A28)

conserve (kən sûrv′) To save, protect, or use something wisely without wasting it. (p. C34)

consumer (kən sü′mər) An organism that eats producers or other consumers. (pp. A40, B17)

crater (krā′tər) A hollow area in the ground. (p. D49)

cutting (kut′ing) A plant part from which a new plant can grow. (p. A30)

cytoplasm (sī′tə pla′zəm) A clear, jellylike material that fills both plant and animal cells. (p. A10)

D

decibel (dB) (des′ə bel′) A unit that measures loudness. (p. F69)

decomposer (dē′kəm pō′zər) An organism that breaks down dead plant and animal material. *Decomposers* recycle chemicals so they can be used again. (p. B18)

define based on observations (di fīn′ bāst ôn ob′zər vā′shənz) To put together a description that relies on examination and experience. (p. S7)

degree (di grē′) The unit of measurement for temperature. (p. F43)

PRONUNCIATION KEY

a at; ā ape; ä far; âr care; ô law; e end; ē me; i it; ī ice; îr pierce; o hot; ō old; ôr fork; oi oil; ou out; u up; ū use; ü rule; u̇ pull; ûr turn; hw white; ng song; th thin; th this; zh measure; ə about, taken, pencil, lemon, circus

desert (dez′ərt) A hot dry place with very little rain. (p. B55)

development (di vel′əp mənt) The way a living thing changes during its life. (p. A6)

distance (dis′təns) The length between two places. (p. E7)

E

earthquake (ûrth′kwāk) A sudden movement in the rocks that make up Earth's crust. (p. C72)

ecosystem (ek′ō sis′təm) All the living and nonliving things in an environment and all their interactions. (p. B6)

electric current (i lek′trik kûr′ənt) Electricity that flows through a circuit. (p. F72)

element (el′ə mənt) A building block of matter. (p. F28)

embryo (em′brē ō) A young organism that is just beginning to grow. (p. A26)

endangered (en dān′jərd) Close to becoming extinct; having very few of its kind left. (p. B64)

energy (en′ər jē) The ability to do work. (pp. A18, E39)

energy pyramid (en′ər jē pir′ə mid′) A diagram that shows how energy is used in an ecosystem. (p. B22)

environment (en vī′rən mənt) The things that make up an area, such as land, water, and air. (p. A8)

erosion (i rō′zhən) The carrying away of weathered materials. (p. C62)

evaporate (i vap′ə rāt′) v. To change from a liquid to a gas. (pp. C31, F17) —**evaporation** (i vap′ə rā′shən′) n. (p. D17)

experiment (ek sper′ə ment′) To perform a test to support or disprove a hypothesis. (p. S7)

extinct (ek stingkt) Died out, leaving no more of that type of organism alive. (p. B66)

F

fertilizer (fûr′tə līz) A substance added to the soil that is used to make plants grow. (p. C42)

first quarter (fûrst kwôr′tər) A phase of the Moon in which the right half is visible and growing larger. (p. D47)

fish (fish) An animal that lives its whole life in water. (p. A71)

flood (flud) A great rush of water over usually dry land. (p. C71)

flowering plant (flou'ər ing plant) A plant that produces seeds inside of flowers. (p. A28)

food chain (füd chān) A series of organisms that depend on one another for food. (p. B17)

food web (füd web) Several food chains that are connected. (p. B20)

force (fôrs) A push or pull, such as the one that moves a lever. (pp. E14, E44)

form a hypothesis (fôrm ə hī poth'ə sis) To make a statement that can be tested in answer to a question. (p. S7)

fossil (fos'əl) The imprint or remains of something that lived long ago. (p. C22)

freeze (frēz) To turn from water to ice. (p. F17)

friction (frik'shən) A force that occurs when one object rubs against another. (p. E26)

fuel (fū'əl) A substance burned for its energy. (p. C26)

fulcrum (fŭl'krəm) The point where a lever turns or pivots. (p. E44)

full Moon (fŭl mün) or **second quarter** (sek'ənd kwôr'tər) The phase of the Moon in which all of its sunlit half is visible from Earth. (p. D47)

fungi, (fun'jī) *pl. n., sing.* **fungus** (fung'gəs) One- or many-celled organisms that absorb food from dead organisms. (p. B18)

G

gas (gas) Matter that has no definite shape or volume. (p. F14)

germinate (jûr'mə nāt) To begin to grow, as when the right conditions allow a seed to develop. (p. A26)

PRONUNCIATION KEY

a at; ā ape; ä far; âr care; ô law; e end; ē me; i it; ī ice; îr pierce; o hot; ō old; ôr fork; oi oil; ou out; u up; ū use; ü rule; ù pull; ûr turn; hw white; ng song; th thin; <u>th</u> this; zh measure; ə about, taken, pencil, lemon, circus

glacier (glā'shər) A large mass of ice in motion. (p. C62)

gram (gram) A metric unit used to measure mass; 1,000 *grams* equals 1 kilogram. (p. F9)

gravity (grav'i tē) A pulling force between two objects, such as Earth and you. (p. E16)

groundwater (ground wô'tər) Water stored in the cracks of underground rocks and soil. (p. C33)

H

habitat (hab'i tat) The home of a living thing. (p. B7)

heat (hēt) A form of energy that makes things warmer. (p. F42)

herbivore (hûr'bə vôr') An animal that eats only plants. (p. B20)

heredity (hə red'i tē) The passing of traits from parents to offspring. (p. A27)

hibernate (hī'bər nāt') To rest or sleep through the cold winter. (p. A46)

host (hōst). An organism that a parasite lives with. (p. B31)

humus (hü'məs) Leftover decomposed plant and animal matter. (p. C14)

hurricane (hûr'i kān') A violent storm with strong winds and heavy rains. (p. C70)

I

igneous rock (ig'nē əs rok) A "fire-made" rock formed from melted rock material. (p. C8)

imprint (im'print') A shallow mark or print in a rock. (p. C23)

inclined plane (in klīnd' plān) A flat surface that is raised at one end. (p. E54)

infer (in fûr') To form an idea from facts or observations. (p. S7)

inherited trait (in her'i təd trāt) A characteristic that comes from your parents. (p. A56)

inner planet (in'ər plan'it) Any of the four planets in the solar system that are closest to the Sun: Mercury, Venus, Earth, and Mars. (p. D56)

insulator (in'sə lā'tər) A material that heat doesn't travel through easily. (p. F46)

interpret data (in tûr′prit dā′tə) To use the information that has been gathered to answer questions or solve a problem. (p. S7)

K

key (kē) A table that shows what different symbols on a map stand for. (p. E10)

kilogram (kil′ə gram′) A metric unit used to measure mass; 1 *kilogram* equals 1,000 grams. (p. F9)

L

landform (land′fôrm′) A feature on Earth's surface. (p. C54)

last quarter (last kwôr′tər) or **third quarter** (thûrd kwôr′tər) The phase of the waning Moon in which the left half is visible but growing smaller. (p. D47)

leaf (lēf) A plant part that grows from the stem and helps the plant get air and make food. (p. A18)

learned trait (lûrnd trāt) Something that you are taught or learn from experience. (p. A56)

lens (lenz) A curved piece of glass. (p. D58)

lever (lev′ər) A straight bar that moves on a fixed point. (p. E44)

life cycle (līf sī′kəl) All the stages in an organism's life. (p. A26)

liquid (lik′wid) Matter that has a definite volume but not a definite shape. (p. F14)

liter (lē′tər) A metric unit used to measure volume. (p. F9)

load (lōd) The object that a lever lifts or moves. (p. E44)

loam (lōm) A kind of soil that contains clay, sand, silt, and humus. Plants grow well in loam. (p. C15)

luster (lus′tər) How an object reflects light. (p. F6)

PRONUNCIATION KEY

a **at**; ā **ape**; ä **far**; âr **care**; ô **law**; e **end**; ē **me**; i **it**; ī **ice**; îr **pierce**; o **hot**; ō **old**; ôr **fork**; oi **oil**; ou **out**; u **up**; ū **use**; ü **rule**; u̇ **pull**; ûr **turn**; hw **white**; ng **song**; th **thin**; th **this**; zh **measure**; ə **about, taken, pencil, lemon, circus**

machine (mə shēn´) A tool that makes work easier to do. (p. E44)

magnetism (mag´ni tiz´əm) The property of an object that makes it attract iron. (p. F26)

make a model (māk ə mod´əl) To make something to represent an object or event. (p. S7)

mammal (mam´əl) An animal with fur that feeds its young with milk. (p. A74)

map (map) A flat drawing that shows the positions of things. (p. E10)

mass (mas) The amount of matter in an object. (p. F7)

matter (mat´ər) Anything that takes up space and has mass. (pp. D16, F6)

measure (mezh´ər) To find the size, volume, area, mass, weight, or temperature of an object, or how long an event occurs. (p. S7)

melt (melt) To change from a solid to a liquid. (p. F17)

metal (met´əl) A shiny material found in the ground. (p. F26)

metamorphic rock (met´ə môr´fik rok) A rock that has changed form through squeezing and heating. (p. C9)

metamorphosis (met´ə môr´fə sis) A change in the body form of an organism. (p. A52)

microscope (mī´krə skōp´) A device that uses glass lenses to allow people to see very small things. (p. A10)

migrate (mī´grāt) To move to another place. (p. A46)

mimicry (mim´i krē) The imitation by one animal of the traits of another. (p. B53)

mineral (min´ə rəl) A naturally occurring substance, neither plant nor animal. (pp. A16, C6)

mixture (miks´chər) Different types of matter mixed together. The properties of each kind of matter in the mixture does not change. (p. F18)

mold (mold) An empty space in a rock that once contained an object such as a dead organism. (p. C23)

motion (mō´shən) A change in position. (p. E8)

mountain (moun′tən) The highest of Earth's landforms. *Mountains* often have steep sides and pointed tops. (p. C55)

N

natural resource (nach′ər əl rē′sôrs′) A material on Earth that is necessary or useful to people. (p. C38)

nectar (nek′tər) The sugary liquid in flowers that lures insects that aid in pollination. (p. A28)

new Moon (nü mün) A phase of the Moon in which none of its sunlit half is visible from Earth. (p. D47)

newton (nü′tən) The unit used to measure pushes and pulls. (pp. E17, F10)

niche (nich) The job or role an organism has in an ecosystem. (p. B44)

nonrenewable resource (non′ri nü′ə bəl rē′sôrs′) A resource that cannot be reused or replaced easily. (p. C41)

nucleus (nü′klē əs) The control center of a cell. (p. A11)

O

observe (əb sûrv′) To use one or more of the senses to identify or learn about an object or event. (p. S7)

omnivore (om′nə vôr′) An animal that eats both plants and animals. (p. B21)

opaque (ō pāk′) A material that doesn't allow light to pass through. (p. F54)

orbit (ôr′bit) The path an object follows as it revolves around another object. (p. D38)

organ (ôr′gən) A group of tissues that work together. (p. A62)

PRONUNCIATION KEY

a at; ā ape; ä far; âr care; ô law; e end; ē me; i it; ī ice; îr pierce; o hot; ō old; ôr fork; oi oil; ou out; u up; ū use; ü rule; u̇ pull; ûr turn; hw white; ng song; th thin; th this; zh measure; ə about, taken, pencil, lemon, circus

organism (ôr'gə niz'əm) Any living thing. (p. A6)

outer planet (out'ər plan'it) Any of the five planets in the solar system that are farthest from the Sun: Jupiter, Saturn, Uranus, Neptune, and Pluto. (p. D56)

oxygen (ok'sə jən) A gas that is in air and water. (p. A19)

P

parasite (par'ə sīt'). An organism that lives in or on a host. (p. B31)

perish (per'ish) To fail to survive. (p. B63)

phase (fāz) An apparent change in the Moon's shape. (p. D46)

physical change (fiz'i kəl chānj) A change in the way matter looks that leaves the matter itself unchanged. (p. F16)

pitch (pich) How high or low a sound is. (p. F66)

plain (plān) Wide flat lands. (p. C55)

planet (plan'it) Any of the nine large bodies that orbit the Sun. In order from the Sun outward, they are Mercury, Venus, Earth, Mars, Jupiter, Saturn, Uranus, Neptune, and Pluto. (p. D54)

pollen (pol'ən) A powdery material needed by the eggs of flowers to make seeds. (p. A28)

pollution (pə lü'shən) The adding of harmful substances to the water, air, or land. (p. C42)

population (pop'yə lā'shən) All the members of a single type of organism in an ecosystem. (p. B6)

position (pə zish'ən) The location of an object. (p. E6)

precipitation (pri sip'i tā'shən) Water in the atmosphere that falls to Earth as rain, snow, hail, or sleet. (p. D19)

predator (pred'ə tər) An animal that hunts for food. (p. B28)

predict (pri dikt') To state possible results of an event or experiment. (p. S7)

prey (prā) The animals that predators eat. (p. B28)

prism (pri'zəm) A thick piece of glass that refracts light. (p. F57)

producer (prə dü'sər) An organism such as a plant that makes its own food. (p. B16)

property (prop'ər tē) Any characteristic of matter that you can observe. (p. F6)

pulley (pùl'ē) A simple machine that uses a wheel and a rope. (p. E48)

R

rain gauge (rān gāj) A device that measures how much precipitation has fallen. (p. D24)

ramp (ramp) Another name for an inclined plane. (p. E54)

recycle (rē sī'kəl) To treat something so it can be used again. (p. C44)

reduce (ri düs') To use less of something. (p. C44)

reflect (ri flekt') The bouncing of light off a surface. (p. F55)

refract (ri frakt') The bending of light as it passes through matter. (p. F56)

relocate (rē lō'kāt) To find a new home. (p. B63)

renewable resource (ri nü'ə bəl rē'sôrs') A resource that can be replaced or used over and over again. (p. C40)

reproduction (rē'prə duk'shən) The way organisms make more of their own kind. (p. A7)

reptile (rep'təl') An animal that lives on land and has waterproof skin. (p. A72)

reservoir (rez'ər vwär') A storage area for fresh water supplies. (p. C32)

respond (ri spond') To react to changes in the environment. (p. A8)

reuse (rē ūz') *v.* To use something again. (p. C44)

revolve (ri volv') To move around another object. (p. D38)

PRONUNCIATION KEY

a at; ā ape; ä far; âr care; ô law; e end; ē me; i it; ī ice; îr pierce; o hot; ō old; ôr fork; oi oil; ou out; u up; ū use; ü rule; ù pull; ûr turn; hw white; ng song; th thin; <u>th</u> this; zh measure; ə about, taken, pencil, lemon, circus

river (riv′ər) A large stream of water that flows across the land. (p. C55)

root (rüt) A plant part that takes in water and grows under the ground. (p. A17)

rotate (rō′tāt) To turn around. (p. D36)

S

sand dune (sand dün) A mound of windblown sand. (p. C55)

sapling (sap′ling) A very young tree. (p. A6)

satellite (sat′ə līt′) Any object that orbits another larger body in space. (p. D46)

scavenger (skav′ən jər) An animal that gets its food by eating dead organisms. (p. B29)

screw (skrü) An inclined plane wrapped into a spiral. (p. E56)

sedimentary rock (sed′ə men′tə rē rok) A kind of rock formed when sand, mud, pebbles at the bottom of rivers, lakes, and oceans pile up. (p. C8)

seedling (sēd′ling) A young plant. (p. A27)

shelter (shel′tər) A place or object that protects an animal and keeps It safe. (p. A44)

silt (silt) Soil that is made of tiny rocks. *Silt* is carried by water and deposited as sediment. (p. C14)

simple machine (sim′pəl mə shēn′) A machine with few or no moving parts. (p. E44)

soil (soil) A mixture of tiny rock particles, minerals, and decayed plant and animal materials. (p. C14)

solar system (sō′lər sis′təm) The Sun and all the objects that orbit the Sun. (p. D54)

solid (sol′id) Matter that has a definite shape and volume. (p. F14)

solution (sə lü′shən) A kind of mixture in which one or more types of matter are mixed evenly in another kind of matter. (p. F19)

speed (spēd) How fast an object moves over a certain distance. (p. E9)

sphere (sfîr) A body that has the shape of a ball or globe. (p. D36)

spore (spôr) One of the tiny reproductive bodies of ferns and mosses, similar to the seeds of other plants. (p. A30)

star (stär) A huge, hot sphere of gases, like the Sun, that gives off its own light. (p. D55)

stem (stem) A plant part that supports the plant. (p. A17)

switch (swich) A lever that opens or closes an electric circuit. (p. F73)

system (sis'təm) A group of parts that work together. (p. A62)

T

telescope (tel'ə skōp') A tool that gathers light to make faraway objects appear closer. (p. D58)

temperature (tem'pər ə cher) How hot or cold something is. (pp. D8, F43)

texture (teks'chər) How the surface of an object feels to the touch. (p. F6)

thermometer (thər mom'ə tər) An instrument used to measure temperature. (pp. D8, D24)

tissue (tish'ü) A group of cells that are alike. (p. A62)

tornado (tôr nā'dō) A violent, whirling wind that moves across the ground in a narrow path. (p. C70)

tuber (tü'bər) The underground stem of a plant such as the potato. (p. A30)

tundra (tun'drə) A cold dry place. (p. B55)

U

use numbers (ūz num'bərz) To order, count, add, subtract, multiply, and divide to explain data. (p. S7)

use variables (ūz vâr'ē ə bəlz) To identify and separate things in an experiment that can be changed or controlled. (p. S7)

PRONUNCIATION KEY

a at; ā ape; ä far; âr care; ô law; e end; ē me; i it; ī ice; îr pierce; o hot; ō old; ôr fork; oi oil; ou out; u up; ū use; ü rule; ủ pull; ûr turn; hw white; ng song; th thin; <u>th</u> this; zh measure; ə about, taken, pencil, lemon, circus

valley (val′ē) An area of low land lying between hills or mountains. (p. C55)

vibrate (vī′brāt) To move back and forth quickly. (p. F64)

volcano (vol kā′nō) An opening in the surface of Earth. (p. C73)

volume (vol′ūm) **1.** A measure of how much space matter takes up. (p. F7) **2.** How loud or soft a sound is. (p. F67)

W

water cycle (wô′tər sī′kəl) The movement of Earth's water over and over from a liquid to a gas and from a gas to a liquid. (pp. C31, D19)

water vapor (wô′tər vā′pər) Water in the form of a gas in Earth's atmosphere. (p. D17)

weather (we<u>th</u>′ər) The condition of the atmosphere at a given time and place. (p. D6)

weather vane (we<u>th</u>′ər vān) A device that indicates the direction of the wind. (p. D25)

weathering (we<u>th</u>′ər ing) The process that causes rocks to crumble, crack, and break. (p. C60)

wedge (wej) Two inclined planes placed back to back. (p. E55)

weight (wāt) The measure of the pull of gravity between an object and Earth. (p. E17)

wheel and axle (hwēl and ak′səl) A wheel that turns on a post. (p. E47)

wind (wind) Moving air. (p. D10)

windlass (wind′ləs) A wheel and axle machine that is turned by a hand crank to lift a bucket in a well. (p. E47)

work (wûrk) The force that changes the motion of an object. (p. E38)

Index

* Indicates an activity related to this topic.

* Indicates an activity related to this topic.

* Indicates an activity related to this topic.

* Indicates an activity related to this topic.

* Indicates an activity related to this topic.

Threads of a screw – Writing link

* Indicates an activity related to this topic.

Credits

Page placement key: (t) top, (tr) top right, (tl) top left, (tm) top middle, (tml) top middle left, (tmr) top middle right, (m) middle, (l) left, (ml) middle left,(r) right, (mr) middle right,(b) bottom, (br) bottom right,(bl) bottom left, (bm) bottom middle, (bml) bottom middle left, (bmr) bottom middle right, (bg) background, (i) inset, (ti) top inset, (bi) bottom inset

Cover Design and Illustration: Robert Brook Allen

Cover Photos: Kim Taylor/Bruce Coleman/Natural Selection, (bg) Darrell Gulin/Stone, (l) © PhotoSpin 2000

Illustrations: Dolores Bego: p. E10; Frank Comito: p. R6; Barbara Cousins: pp. E21, R25, R27, (l) R28, R29; Daniel DelValle: p. B5; Jeff Fagen: pp. E27, E33; Function Through Form: p. F29; Peter Gunther: pp. C14,C26, C30, C31, C33, C61, C73, D7, D8, D10, D18, D31, D40, D42, E17, F8, F15, F42, F57, F63, F72; Colin Hayes: pp. A41, E44, E48, E48, E54, E55, E60, E61, R5, R7, R9, R16, R17, R18, (l) R19; John Karapelou: pp. R30, R32, (m) R33, (b) R33; Yuan Lee: B7, B8, B16, F68, F77; Tom Leonard: pp. R20,R21, R22, R23; Kevin O'Malley: pp. E25, F10, F11; Joe LeMonnier: pp. B64, C56, D11, D13, D26, D36, D37, D47, D61; Steve Oh: pp. A62, R26, R27, (r) R28, R29, R31, R34; Sharon O'Neil: p. C47; Precision Graphics: pp. A28, A29, A42, A71; Pat Rasch: pp. E56, E57, E58; Molly Scanlon: pp. F7, F64, F66, F74; Rob Schuster: p. F73; Neecy Twinem: pp. B10, B20; Olivia: pp. R2, R3, R9, R10, R11, R14, R15, (r) R19; Patricia Wynne: pp. S4, S5, R24, (t) R33; J/B Woolsey Associates: pp. A10, A11, C54, C76; Josie Yee: pp. D38, D54.

Photography Credits: All photographs are by the Macmillan/McGraw-Hill School Division (MMSD) and Michael Groen, Dan Howell, Ken Karp, Dave Mager, John Serafin for MMSD except as noted below.

Contents: iv: Photodisc. v: (l) Runk/Schoenberger/Grant Heilman Photography, Inc.; (r) Photodisc. vi: (l) Francois Gohier/Photo Researchers, Inc.; (r) American Museum of Natural History. vii: (l) NASA/Photo Researchers, Inc.; (r) John Sanford/Photo Researchers, Inc. viii: Peter Weimann/Animals Animals. ix: D. Boone/Corbis.

National Geographic Invitation to Science: S1: (bg) Greig Cranna/Stock • Boston; (i) Mark A. Madison. S2: Mark A. Madison. S3: (t) NASA/Peter Arnold Inc.; (b) Mark A. Madison. S7: Ken Karp. S8: (br) PhotoDisc.

National Geographic Unit Opener A: A0: Clive Druett/Papilio/Corbis. A1: Victoria McCormick/Animals Animals. **Unit A:** A2: Alan Oddie/PhotoEdit. A4: Douglas Peebles/Corbis. A5: Ken Karp. A6: (t) Terry Eggers/The Stock Market; (l) Tony Wharton/Corbis; (r) The Stock Market; (b) Terry Eggers/The Stock Market. A7: (t) Frank Siteman/Stock • Boston; (tr) Photodisc; (mr) Photodisc; (br) Photodisc. A8: (t) Gerard Fuehrer/DRK Photo; SuperStock. A9: (tl) Norbert Wu/Peter Arnold Inc.; (tr) Secret Sea Visions/Peter Arnold Inc.; (b) Joe McDonald/Visuals Unlimited. A10: (t) Kent Wood/Photo Researchers, Inc.; (b) Dwight R. Kuhn. A11: (t) Ken Karp; (b) Moredun Animal Health LTD/Science Photo Library/Photo Researchers, Inc. A12: Ken Karp. A13: Cart Roessler/Animals Animals. A14: (bg) PhotoDisc.; (tl) Doug Peebles/Panoramic Images; (tr) Allen Prier/Panoramic Images; (m) Mark Segal/Panoramic Images. A15: Ken Karp. A16: (bg) Runk/Schoenberger/Grant Heilman Photography; (i) E. Webber/Visuals Unlimited. A17: (l) Jim Zipp/Photo Researchers, Inc.; (r) Jenny Hager/The Image Works. A18: (l) Runk/Schoenberger/Grant Heilman Photography; (r) C.G. Van Dyke/Visuals Unlimited. A19: (l) Dave M. Phillips/Visuals Unlimited; (b) Ken Karp. A20: (t) Bill Beatty/Visuals Unlimited; (b) Pat O'Hara/DRK Photo. A22: (bg) Randy Green/FPG International; (l) Stan Osolinski/Dembinsky Photo Assoc.; (r) Larry West/FPG International. A23: (t) John M. Roberts/The Stock Market; (b) J. H. Robinson/Photo Researchers, Inc. A24: Neil Gilchrist/Panoramic Images. A25: Ken Karp. A26: (t) D. Gavagnaro/Visuals Unlimited; (tm) Kevin Collins/Visuals Unlimited; (bm) Tony Freeman/PhotoEdit; (bl) Inga Spence/Tom Stack & Associates; (br) Inga Spence/Visuals Unlimited. A27: D. Gavagnaro/Visuals Unlimited. A29: Gerald and Buff Corsi/Visuals Unlimited. A30: (t) David Young-Wolfe/PhotoEdit; (m) David Young-Wolfe/PhotoEdit; (bl) Ed Reschke/Peter Arnold Inc.; (br) Jeff J. Daly/Visuals Unlimited. A31: Inga Spence/Visuals Unlimited. A32: Ed Galindo. A33: (t) Ed Galindo; (b) C Squared Studios/PhotoDisc. A36: Stephen J. Krasemann/Photo Researchers, Inc. A38: Jade Albert/FPG International. A39: Ken Karp. A40: (t) Fritz Polikng/Bruce Coleman Inc.; (bl) Joe McDonald/DRK Photo; (br) Dale E. Boyer/Photo Researchers, Inc. A41: Kevin Schafer/Peter Arnold Inc. A42: (i) W. Gregory Brown/Animals Animals; (t) Ken Karp; (b) Michael S. Nolan/Tom Stack & Associates. A43: (t) Eric & David Hosking/Corbis; (m) John Cancalosi/DRK Photo; (b) Ted Levine/Animals Animals. A45: (t) Zoran Milich/Allsport USA; (b) Mark Newman/Bruce

Coleman Inc. A46: (t) David Madison/Bruce Coleman Inc.; (m) Runk/Schoenberger/Grant Heilman Photography; (b) John Cancalosi/DRK Photo. A48: (bg) Ken Lucas/Visuals Unlimited; (t) Skip Moody/Dembinsky Photo Assoc.; (b) Skip Moody/Dembinsky Photo Assoc. A49: (tl) Skip Moody/Dembinsky Photo Assoc.; (tr) Skip Moody/Dembinsky Photo Assoc.; (m) Jon Dicus; (b) Skip Moody/Dembinsky Photo Assoc. A50: Tim Davis/Photo Researchers, Inc. A51: Ken Karp. A52: (t) Dwight R. Kuhn; (b) Arthur Morris/Visuals Unlimited. A53: (tl) Gelnn M. Oliver/Visuals Unlimited; (tr) Robert P. Carr/Bruce Coleman Inc.; (tm) Pat Lynch/Zipp/Photo Researchers, Inc.; (ml) Nuridsany et Perennou/Zipp/Photo Researchers, Inc.; (mr) Robert L. Dunne/Bruce Coleman Inc.; (bl) Sharon Cummings/Dembinsky Photo Assoc.; (br) John Mielcarek/Dembinsky Photo Assoc. A54: (t) SuperStock; (mr) Lynn Rogers/Peter Arnold Inc.; (bl) Erwin and Peggy Bauer/Bruce Coleman Inc.; (br) Pat and Tom Leeson/Photo Researchers, Inc. A55: (t) Cabisco/Visuals Unlimited; (ml) E.A. Janes/Bruce Coleman Inc; (mr) Lindholm/Visuals Unlimited; (bm) Fred Breummer/DRK Photo; (bl) M H Sharp/Photo Researchers, Inc; (br) Dave B. Fleetham/Visuals Unlimited. A56: (t) Ken Karp; (bl) George Shelley/The Stock Market; (br) Richard Hutchings/PhotoEdit. A58: (bg) J.C. Carton/Bruce Coleman Inc.; (i) Bill Banaszewski/Visuals Unlimited. A60: Robert Maier/Animals Animals. A61: Ken Karp. A62: (t) Ken Karp; (b) M.I. Walker/Science Source/Photo Researchers, Inc. A63: (t) R. Dowling/Animals Animals; (b) Joe McDonald/Animals Animals. A64: (t) Robert Winslow; (b) Tom Brakefield/Corbis. A65: (t) James Watt/Animals Animals; (b) Jeff Rotman/Jeff Rotman Photography. A66: Photodisc. A68: VCG/FPG International. A69: (t) Stephen Dalton/Animals Animals; (tm) Tony Wharton/Corbis; (m) G.W.Willis/Animals Animals; (ml) Eye Wire; (mr) Brian Parker/Tom Stack & Associates; (bl) Kichen and Hurst/Tom Stack & Associates; (br) Lisa and Mike Husar/DRK Photo. A70: (l) Darryl Torckler/Tony Stone Images; (r) Rob Simpson/Visuals Unlimited. A71: (i) George Bernard/Animals Animals; (t) Breck P. Kent/Animals Animals. A72: (t) Jane Borton/Bruce Coleman Inc.; (b) E.R. Degginger/Animals Animals. A73: (l) S. Nielson/DRK Photo; (r) Robert Winslow. A74: (t) Jeff Rotman/Jeff Rotman Photography; (b) Dave Watts/Tom Stack & Associates. A75: (t) Erwin & Peggy Bauer/Bruce Coleman Inc.; (b) Lynn M. Stone/Bruce Coleman Inc. A77: (l) SuperStock; (r) SuperStock. A78: (bg) Michael Fogden/DRK Photo; (i) Dr. Fransisco Gomez-Dallmeier. A80: (tl) David Young-Wolfe/PhotoEdit; (tr) Jeff J. Daly/Visuals Unlimited.

National Geographic Unit Opener B: B00: Tim Flach/Tony Stone. B0 Christer Fredriksson/Natural Selection Stock Photography. B1 Tim Davis/Tony Stone. **Unit B:** B2: (bg) Corbis, (l) John Gerlach/Visuals Unlimited; (m) David M. Schleser/Photo Researchers, Inc.; (r) Tony Stone Images. B4: Johnny Johnson/Animals Animals. B5: Photodisc. B6: (t) Nicholas DeVore/Tony Stone Images; (b) Joseph Van Os/Image Bank. B12: (i) Lance Nelson/The Stock Market; (m) Jeff Greenberg/Visuals Unlimited; (b) Jeff Greenberg/PhotoEdit. B13: (i) Photodisc; (t) Gerard Lacz/Peter Arnold Inc.; (b) PhotoDisc. B14: (bg) L. Lenz/Natural Selection. B16: Kim Taylor/Dorling Kindersley Ltd. B18: (i) Runk/Schoenberger /Grant Heilman Photography; (t) SuperStock; (bl) Tom Bean/DRK Photo; (br) Kim Taylor/Dorling Kindersley Ltd. B19: (l) Michael P. Gadomski/Photo Researchers, Inc. B22: (t) John Warden/Tony Stone Images; (tm) Tom J. Ulrich/Visuals Unlimited; (bm) John Shaw/Bruce Coleman Inc; (b) Runk/Schoenberger/Grant Heilman Photography, Inc. B23: Jim Steinberg/Photo Researchers, Inc. B24: (bg) Michael Simpson/FPG International. B26: (bg) Kent Foster/Photo Researchers, Inc; (i) William H. Mullins/Photo Researchers, Inc. B28: (ti) John Shaw/Bruce Coleman Inc.; (t) Kim Taylor/Dorling Kindersley Ltd.; (tm) Kim Taylor/Dorling Kindersley Ltd.; (ml) Arthur Morris/The Stock Market.; (mr) M. C. Chamberlain/DRK Photo; (b) Kim Taylor/Dorling Kindersley Ltd. B29: (t) Jeremy Woodhouse/PhotoDisc; (b) Jerry Young/Dorling Kindersley Ltd. B30: (tl) Nawrocki Stock Photo; (b) Carl Roessler/Bruce Coleman Inc. B31: (t) S. Dimmitt/Photo Researchers, Inc; (m) James H. Robinson/Photo Researchers, Inc.; (bl) Tony Stone Images; (br) Runk/Schoenberger/Grant Heilman Photography, Inc. B32: (r) Kim Taylor/Dorling Kindersley Ltd. B34: (bg) John Elk III; (ti) Trevor Barrett/Earth Scenes; (bi) George D. Lepp/Photo Researchers, Inc. B35: Kjell B. Sandved/Visuals Unlimited. B37: (l) Runk/Schoenberger/Grant Heilman Photography, Inc.; (m) Runk/Schoenberger/Grant Heilman Photography, Inc; (r) Arthur Morris/Visuals Unlimited. B38: Robert Winslow. B40: (bg) The Stock Market. B42: (t) Stephen Dalton/Animals Animals; (b) Richard Day/Panoramic Images. B43: (tl) Steve Maslowski/Visuals Unlimited; (tr) James P. Rowan/DRK Photo; (tr) George D. Dodge/Bruce Coleman Inc.; (br) Michael Dwyer/Stock • Boston. B44: (t) Gail Shumway/FPG International; (b) Ken Karp. B45: (l) Ken Lax/Photo Researchers, Inc. B46: (t) M.L. Sinibaldi/The Stock Market; (b) H.P. Merten/The Stock Market. B47: Larry Ulrich/DRK Photo. B48: (bg) Johnny Johnson/DRK Photo; (t) Tom and Pat Leeson/DRK Photo; (b) Richard &Susan Day/Animals Animals. B50: (t) Gail Shumway/FPG International; (m) Jack Jeffrey/Photo Resource Hawaii.; (b) John Cancalosi/DRK Photo. B51: (tl) Francis/Donna

Caldwell/Visuals Unlimited; (tr) Jack Hollingsworth/Photodisc; (b) Kim Taylor/Bruce Coleman Inc. B52: (t) Gregory Ochoki/Photo Researchers, Inc.; (b) Breck P. Kent/Animals Animals. B53: (t) Stephen J. Krasemann/DRK Photo; (m) A. Cosmos Blank/Photo Researchers, Inc.; (b) John Eastcott/Yva Momatiuk/DRK Photo. B54: (t) Zig Leszcynski/Animals Animals; (m) MIchael Fogden/DRK Photo; (b) MIchael Fogden/DRK Photo. B55: (tl) Pat O'Hara/DRK Photo; (tr) Richard Kolar/Animals Animals; (tm) Don Enger/Animals Animals; (bl) Jim Steinberg/Photo Researchers, Inc.; (br) Stephen J. Krasemann/Photo Researchers, Inc. B56: Ken Karp. B57: Chris Johns/National Geographic. B58: (bg) Gary Braasch/Corbis. B59: Ken Karp. B60: (t) Charles Palek/Earth Scenesphic; (b) Pat and Tom Lesson/Photo Researchers, Inc. B61: (l) Robert Madden/National Geographicphic.; (r) Jim Hughes/Visuals Unlimited. B62: (t) Diana L. Stratton/Tom Stack & Associates; (tm) Doug Sokell/Visuals Unlimited; (l) Kent and Donna Dannen/Photo Researchers, Inc.; (bm) Sharon Gerig/Tom Stack & Associates; (b) Pat and Tom Lesson/DRK Photo. B63: (t) Joe & Carol McDonald/Visuals Unlimited; (b) Stephen J. Krasemann/DRK Photo. B64: (t) M.C. Chamberlain/DRK Photo; (bl) Erwin and Peggy Bauer/Bruce Coleman Inc.; (br) G. Prance/Visuals Unlimited. B65: (b) M.C. Chamberlain/DRK Photo. B66: (t) Stephen J. Krasemann/DRK Photo; (b) Science VU/Visuals Unlimited. B67: Barbara Gerlach/Visuals Unlimited. B69: (l) Pat and Tom Lesson/Photo Researchers, Inc.; (r) Robert Madden/National Geographic. B70: (t) Christina Allen. B71: Myleen Ferguson/PhotoEdit.

National Geographic Unit Opener C: C0: Donovan Reese/Tony Stone. C1: David Muench/Tony Stone. **Unit C:** C2: David Muench/Corbis. C4: (bg) Chip Porter/Tony Stone Images. C5: Ken Karp. C6: (t) Joyce Photographics/Photo Researchers, Inc.; (m) Runk/Schoenberger/Grant Heilman Photography; (b) Bill Bachmann/Index Stock Imagery. C7: (t) Tom Pantages; (m) Tom Pantages; (b) Ken Karp. C8: Adam G. Sylvester/Photo Researchers, Inc. C9: (tl) Ken Karp; (tr) S. Callahan/Visuals Unlimited; (tml) Joyce Photographics/Photo Researchers, Inc.; (tmr) Runk/Schoenberger/Grant Heilman Photography; (bl) Charles R. Belinky/Photo Researchers, Inc.; (br) Ken Karp. C10: (t) Frederik D. Bodin/Stock • Boston; (m) Erich Lessing/Art Resource; (b) Boleslaw Edelhajt/Gamma-Liaison. C12: (b) Bo Brannhage/Panoramic Images. C13: Ken Karp. C14: Larry Lefever/Grant Heilman Photography. C15: (l) Stephen Ogilvy; (m) Ken Karpgilvy; (r) Ken Karp. C16: Ken Karp. C17: (l) George Lepp/Corbis; (r) Runk/Schoenberger/Grant Heilman Photography. C18: (tl) Roy Morsch/The Stock Market; (tr) Roy Morsch/The Stock Market; (m) The National Archives/Corbis; (bm) Roy Morsch/The Stock Market; (b) G. Buttner/Okapia/Photo Researchers, Inc. C19: Arthur C. Smith/Grant Heilman Photography. C20: (bg) Jeff J. Daly/Visuals Unlimited. C21: Ken Karp. C22: Tom Bean/DRK Photo. C23: (t) Runk/Schoenberger/Grant Heilman Photography; (b) Ken Karp. C24: (i) Mehau Kulyk/Photo Researchers, Inc.; (t) Louis Psihoyos/Matrix; (b) Fracois Gohier/Photo Researchers, Inc. C25: (l) Stephen J. Krasemann/DRK Photo; (m) Biophoto Associates/Photo Researchers, Inc.; (r) Stephen J. Krasemann/DRK Photo. C26: Ray Ellis/Photo Researchers, Inc. C28: (bg) F. Stuart Westmorland/Photo Researchers, Inc. C29: Ken Karp. C30: Tom Van Sant/Photo Researchers, Inc. C32: (t) Davis Barber/PhotoEdit; (b) C. C. Lockwood/DRK Photo. C35: John Serafin. C36: (bg) Grant Heilman/Grant Heilman Photography. C37: Ken Karp. C38: (bl) Charles Mauzy/Natural Selection; (br) Emma Lee/Life File/Photodisc. C39: (t) David R. Frazier/Photo Researchers, Inc.; (b) John Elk III. C40: (t) Don and Pat Valenti/DRK Photo; (b) Gary Gray/DRK Photo. C41: (i) Will and Deni McIntyre/Photo Researchers, Inc.; (t) American Museum of Natural History; (b) George Gerster/Photo Researchers, Inc. C42: (t) Ruth Dixon/Stock • Boston; (b) David Ulmer/Stock • Boston. C43: (l) Simon Fraser/Science Photo Library/Photo Researchers, Inc.; (r) Ken Karp. C44: (tl) Larry Lefever/Grant Heilman Photography; (tml) Eye Wire; (tml) R.J. Erwin/DRK Photo; (bl) Tony Freeman/PhotoEdit; (br) Hutchings Photography. C45: (l) Michael P. Gadomski/Photo Researchers, Inc. C46: (t) David Young-Wolfe/PhotoEdit; (b) Chromosohm/Sohm/Stock • Boston. C47: (t) Bonnie Kaman/PhotoEdit; (t) Spencer Grant/PhotoEdit. C50: Addison Geary/Stock • Boston. C52: (bg) Allen Prier/Panoramic Images. C53: (t) Peter Miller/Panoramic Images; (tm) Richard Sisk/Panoramic Images; (m) Mark Heifner/Panoramic Images; (bm) Kim Heacox/Tony Stone Images; (bl) Jack Krawczyk/Panoramic Images; (br) Don Pitcher/Stock • Boston. C56: (tl) Jim Wiebe/Panoramic Images; (tr) Peter Pearson/Tony Stone Images; (bm) Mark Heifner/Panoramic Images; (bl) Richard Sisk/Panoramic Images; (br) Tom Bean/Tony Stone Images. C57: Jack Krawczyk/Panoramic Images. C58: (bg) David L. Brown/Panoramic Images. C59: Ken Karp. C60: (t) Michael P. Gadomski/Photo Researchers, Inc.; (b) John Anderson/Earth Scenes. C61: Ken Karp. C62: (i) Photodisc; (t) Thomas Fletcher/Stock • Boston; (b) Jeff Greenberg/PhotoEdit. C63: Kathy Ferguson/PhotoEdit; (b) Runk/Schoenberger/Grant Heilman Photography. C64: Ken Karp. C65: PhotoEdit. C66: (bg) The National Archives/Corbis; (i) Adam

Jones/Photo Researchers, Inc.; (t) W. E. Ruth/Bruce Coleman Inc. C67: (i) Pat Armstrong/Visuals Unlimited; (m) Sylvan H. Wittaver/Visuals Unlimited; (b) John Sohlden/Visuals Unlimited. C68: (bg) David Young-Wolfe/PhotoEdit. C69: Ken Karp. C70: (t) Ana Laura Gonzalez/Earth Scenes; (b) Art Montes De Oca/FPG International. C72: (t) David Bartruff/FPG International; (b) Will & Deni McIntyre/Photo Researchers, Inc. C73: G. Brad Lewis/Tony Stone Images. C74: (t) David Weintraub/Stock • Boston; (b) Archive photos/Library of Congress. C78: (bg) Fred Bavendam/Peter Arnold Inc.; (t) Dawn Wright/Dawn Wright; (b) Peter Ryan/Scripps Science Photo Library/Photo Researchers, Inc. C79: Mark M. Lawrence/The Stock Market.

National Geographic Unit Opener D: D00: Earth Satellite Corporation/Science Photo Library/Photo Researchers, Inc. D0 John Sanford/Science Photo Library/Photo Researchers, Inc D1: Science Photo Library/Photo Researchers, Inc; Photo Library Int'l/Photo Researchers, Inc. **Unit D:** D2: Jack Krawczyk/Panoramic Images. D4: (bg) Ariel Skelley/The Stock Market. D5: Ken Karp. D6: Ken Karp. D9: (l) Didier Givois/Photo Researchers, Inc.; (r) Ken Karp. D10: David Young-Wolfe/PhotoEdit. D11: Barbara Stotzen/PhotoEdit. D12: Paul & LindaMarie Ambrose/FPG International. D13: Howard Bluestein/Photo Researchers, Inc. D14: (bg) Clifford Paine/Corbis. D15: Ken Karp. D16: (t) Myrleen Ferguson/PhotoEdit; (m) Paul Silverman/Paul Silverman; (b) Michael Newman/PhotoEdit. D17: (t) Diane Hirsch/Fundamental Photographs; (b) Jeff Greenberg/Peter Arnold Inc. D20: Ken Karp. D21: P. Quittemelle/Stock • Boston. D22: (bg) Bob Krist/Corbis. D23: Dave Mager. D24: (tr) Tom Pantages; (t) Tom Pantages; (m) Jeff J. Daly/Stock • Boston. D25: (t) Charles D. Winters/Photo Researchers, Inc.; (br) Ken Karp; (bl) Tony Freeman/PhotoEdit. D27: (b) NOAA/Science photo Library/Photo Researchers, Inc. D28: (t) Michael P. Gadomski/Photo Researchers, Inc.; (b) Michael P. Gadomski/Photo Researchers, Inc. D29: F. Stuart Westmorland/Photo Researchers, Inc. D32: Michael Hovell/Index Stock Imagery. D34: (bg) Robert Mathena/Fundamental Photographs. D35: Ken Karp. D37: (t) Ken Lucas/Visuals Unlimited; (b) Thomas Barbudo/Panoramic Images. D40: Ken Karp. D41: Bob Daemmrich/Stock • Boston. D42: Jim Ballard/All Stock/PNI; David Nunuk/Science Photo Library/Photo Researchers, Inc. D44: (bg) Peter Menzel/Stock • Boston. D45: Ken Karp. D46: John R. Foster/Photo Researchers, Inc. D47: John Sanford/Photo Researchers, Inc. D48: NASA/Science Source/Photo Researchers, Inc. D49: (l) Mark E. Gibson/Visuals Unlimited; (r) NASA/Science Photo Library/Photo Researchers, Inc. D52: (bg) Frank Zullo/Photo Researchers, Inc. D53: Ken Karp. D56: (t) U.S .Geological Survey/Photo Researchers, Inc; (m) NASA/Mark Marten/Photo Researchers, Inc.; (bl) Stock • Boston; (br) NASA/Tom Pantages. D57: (tl) Ross Ressmeyer/NASA/Corbis; (tr) NASA/Photo Researchers, Inc.; (ml) Space Telescope Space Institute/Photo Researchers, Inc.; (mr) NASA/Tom Pantages. D57: (b) Space Telescope Space Institute/Photo Researchers, Inc. D58: (t) Tony Freeman/PhotoEdit; (b) Ken Karp. D62: (bg) Pekka Parvaiainen/Science Photo Library/Photo Researchers, Inc.; (i) Seth Shostak/Seth Shostak. D63: Seth Shostak/Seth Shostak. D64: Ken Karp.

National Geographic Unit Opener E: E0: James Marshall/The Stock Market. E1: Ron Stroud/Masterfile. **Unit E:** E2: Bernard Asset/Photo Researchers, Inc. E4: (bg) S. Dalton/Photo Researchers, Inc. E5: (t) Will Hart/PhotoEdit; (b) Ken Karp. E6: (tl) Gregory K. Scott/Photo Researchers, Inc.; (tr) Foodpix; (ml) Gregory K. Scott/Photo Researchers, Inc.; (mr) Foodpix; (bl) Zoran Milich/Allsport USA; (br) Zoran Milich/Allsport USA. E7: (t) Ken Karp; (b) Ken Karp. E8: (bg) The Stock Market; (t) Robert Winslow; (b) Fritz Polking/Peter Arnold Inc. E9: (t) Joseph Van Os/Image Bank; (b) Peter Weimann/Animals Animals. E12: (bg) Craig J. Brown/Flashfocus. E16: (l) NASA; (r) Hutchings Photography. E17: NASA/Earth Scenes. E18: Photodisc. E19: (t) Art Resource. E20: Ken Karp. E23: (i) Ken Karp. E26: (i) Tony Freeman/PhotoEdit; (b) John Coletti/Stock • Boston. E27: Bob Daemmrich/Stock • Boston. E28: (r) Ken Karp. E30: (bg) Hulton Getty; (l) Michael Conroy/AP World Wide Photos. E31: (t) UPI/Corbis/Bettman; (b) Courtesy of Speedo. E34: Addison Geary/Stock • Boston. E38: (tl) David Young-Wolfe/PhotoEdit; (tr) Hutchings Photography; (bl) Hutchings Photography; (br) John Eastcott/YvaMomatiuk/DRK Photo. E39: (r) Ken Karp; David Matherly/Visuals Unlimited. E42: (b) Bob Daennrich/Stock • Boston. E43: Ken Karp. E45: Ken Karp. E46: (t) Michael Newman/PhotoEdit; (m) Tony Freeman/PhotoEdit; (b) Siede Preis/Photodisc. E47: (t) Roger Wilmshurst; Frank Lane Picture Agency/Corbis; (m) Corbis; (b) Eric Roth/Flashfocus. E48: Ken Karp. E49: (t) Domenicho Fetti/The Granger Collection. E50: (l) Joan Iaconetti/Bruce Coleman Inc.; (r) David Mager. E51: David Mager. E52: (bg) McCutchean/Visuals Unlimited. E54: Richard Hutchings/Photo Researchers, Inc. E55: Donald Specker/Earth Scenes. E56: Mark Burnett/Stock • Boston. E57: (t) Photodisc; (m) Photodisc; (b) David Young-Wolfe/PhotoEdit. E59: Jodi Jacobson. E62: (bg) NASA/The Image Works; (i) Joe Skipper/Archive Photos/Reuters. E63: NASA. E64: (t) Ken Karp; (b) John Neubauer/PhotoEdit.

National Geographic Unit Opener F: F0: SuperStock. F1 Kunio Owaki/The Stock Market. **Unit F:** F2: Myrleen Ferguson/PhotoEdit; (i) Ken Karp; (r) Ken Karp. F6: (t) Hutchings Photography; (m) Photodisc; (ml) RDF/Visuals Unlimited; (mr) RDF/Visuals Unlimited. F7: (l) Spencer Grant/PhotoEdit; (m) Photodisc; (r) Diane Padys/FPG International; (b) Index Stock. F8: (l) Spencer Grant/PhotoEdit; (r) Diane Padys/FPG International. F10: (l) VCG/FPG International; (r) Stock • Boston. F12: (bg) Alan Kearney/FPG International. F13: Ken Karp. F14: (t) PhotoDisc; (bl) PhotoDisc; (br) Hutchings Photography. F15: (l) Hutchings Photography; (m) PhotoDisc; (r) PhotoDisc. F16: (i) Lawrence Migdale; (r) Lawrence Migdale; (b) David Young-Wolfe/PhotoEdit. F17: (tl) SuperStock; (tr) Hutchings Photography; (bl) Amanda Merullo/Stock • Boston; (br) SuperStock. F18: (t) PhotoDisc. F20: Peter Scoones/TCL/Masterfile. F21: (l) Tony Freeman/PhotoEdit. F22: (tl) Ken Karp; (tr) Norman Owen Tomalin/Bruce Coleman Inc.; (tml) Norman Owen Tomalin/Bruce Coleman Inc.; (tmr) Norman Owen Tomalin/Bruce Coleman Inc.; (m) Steve Kline/Bruce Coleman Inc.; (m) Ken Karp; (b) Ken Karp. F23: (t) Norman Owen Tomalin/Bruce Coleman Inc.; (b) Bruce Byers/FPG International. F24: (bg) Spencer Grant/PhotoEdit. F25: Ken Karp. F27: (t) Bo Brannhagen/Panoramic Images; (tm) Burke/Triolo Productions/Foodpix; (m) PhotoDisc; (b) Photodisc. F28: (t) D. Boone/Corbis; (b) Ken Karp. F29: The Stock Market. F30: (l) Photodisc; (m) Eye Wire; (r) PhotoDisc. F31: (bl) PhotoDisc. F32: (t) Ernie Friedlander/Flashfocus; (m) Fred J. Maroon/Photo Researchers, Inc.; (ml) Gabriel Covian/Image Bank; (mr) David Sieren/Visuals Unlimited; (bl) Barbara Stitzer/PhotoEdit. F34: (l) Joel Sartore/Grant Heilman Photography; (r) Leonard Lessin/Peter Arnold Inc.; (b) James L. Amos/Peter Arnold Inc. F35: Gabe Palmer/The Stock Market. F37: Tom Pantages; Richard Megna/Fundamental Photographs; Jerry Driendl/FPG International. F38: Glenn Vanstrum/Earth Scenes. F40: (bg) Tom Bean/DRK Photo; (i) Kim Fennema/Visuals Unlimited. F42: Hutchings Photography. F43: (ti) Hutchings Photography; (bi) Hutchings Photography; (r) Hutchings Photography; (b) Bill Bachmann/PhotoEdit. F44: (l) Hutchings Photography; (b) PhotoDisc. F45: Ken Karp. F46: (t) Jerry Driendl/FPG International; (l) SuperStock; (b) Image Bank. F47: (t) Renee Lynn/Photo Researchers, Inc.; (bl) Nakita Ovsyanikov/Masterfile; (br) SuperStock. F48: (t) Farrel Grehan/Photo Researchers, Inc.; (m) Hutchings Photography; (b) Ken Karp. F49: Nancy P. Alexander/Visuals Unlimited. F50: (bg) Travel Pix/FPG International; (t) Jerome Wexler/Photo Researchers, Inc.; (b) Adam Hart-Davis/Photo Researchers, Inc. F51: (t) Bob Daemmrich/Stock • Boston; (b) FPG International. F52: (bg) Kirchoff/Wohlberg. F53: Ken Karp. F54: (bg) Black Sheep. F55: (b) Gupton/Pictor/Entertainment. F56: (t) Charles D. Winters/Photo Researchers, Inc.; (bl) Hutchings Photography; (br) Photodisc. F57: (i) David Parker/Photo Researchers, Inc.; (b) SuperStock. F58: Ken Karp. F59: (l) Deborah Davis/PhotoEdit; (r) Peter Harholdt/SuperStock. F60: (t) Ken Karp; (t) Jim Cummins/FPG International; (b) Gerald French/FPG International. F61: Frank Krahmer/Bruce Coleman Inc. F62: (bg) Phyllis Picardi/International Stock. F63: Ken Karp. F64: (t) Ken Karp; (b) Spencer Grant/Stock • Boston. F65: (b) Telegraph Colour Library/FPG International. F66: (t) Bill Gallery/Stock • Boston; (b) Corbis. F67: (l) G K & Vikki Hart/Image Bank; (r) David Ducros/Science Photo Library. F68: (l) Chuck Carlton/Flashfocus; (r) Ken Cavanagh/Photo Researchers, Inc. F70: (bg) Chris Minerva/Index Stock Imagery. F71: Ken Karp. F72: Hutchings Photography. F74: (tl) Photodisc; (tr) Hutchings Photography; (ml) Will Crocker/Image Bank; (mr) Will Crocker/Image Bank; (bl) Stephen Marks/Image Bank; (br) Daniel Valdez. F78: (bg) Planet Earth Pictures/FPG International; (i) NASA. F79: Bill Horseman/Stock • Boston.

Science and Health Handbook: R4-R12: Stephen Ogilvy. R13: PhotoDisc. R28-R34: Hutchings Photography.